BYZANTINE POTTERY

KEN DARK

TEMPUS

2001

First published 2001

PUBLISHED IN THE UNITED KINGDOM BY:

Tempus Publishing Ltd
The Mill, Brimscombe Port
Stroud, Gloucestershire GL5 2QG
www.tempus-publishing.com

PUBLISHED IN THE UNITED STATES OF AMERICA BY:

Tempus Publishing Inc.
2 Cumberland Street
Charleston, SC 29401
1-888-313-2665
www.arcadiapublishing.com

Tempus books are available in France and Germany
from the following addresses:

Tempus Publishing Group   Tempus Publishing Group
21 Avenue de la République   Gustav-Adolf-Straße 3
37300 Joué-lès-Tours   99084 Erfurt
FRANCE   GERMANY

British Library Cataloguing in Publication Data.
A catalogue record for this book is available from the British Library.

ISBN 0 7524 1942 0

Typesetting and origination by Tempus Publishing.
PRINTED AND BOUND IN GREAT BRITAIN

Contents

List of illustrations

Cover: Late Byzantine bowl from the Hippodrome of Byzantine Constantinople. *Painting by David Talbot Rice, reproduced with the kind permission of the Talbot Rice family*

Text figures

Colour plates

Preface and acknowledgements

Discussions of the 'end of the Roman Empire' usually focus only on the collapse of imperial control in western Europe, but this was only one half of the Late Roman Empire. By AD 400 the Empire was divided into two parts and while the Western Roman Empire formally ended in the fifth century, the Eastern Roman Empire (known to modern scholars as the 'Byzantine Empire') survived for another millennium. This 'Roman Empire', with its capital city at Constantinople (modern Istanbul), continued to play a central role in political, religious, cultural and economic history throughout the European Middle Ages[1].

The study of pottery plays such a central role in the archaeology of the Western Roman Empire that it comes as a surprise to discover that Byzantine pottery has been largely neglected by archaeologists. In fact, this is the first book to discuss Byzantine pottery as a whole, treating it as a specific category of archaeological data

1 Byzantine pottery from the Great Palace at Constantinople, in The British Museum

and using it to address questions of interpretation beyond the confines of the decoration, date, function and technology of the ceramics themselves.

Earlier studies of this material have examined particular groups of ceramics from a single site or region or belonging to a technical or functional subdivision of the pottery— such as 'glazed wares', 'architectural ceramics', or 'amphorae'. In contrast, this book discusses all Byzantine pottery from the humblest cooking pot to the finest decorated plate. That no such study has hitherto been undertaken of such a large, varied and historically important body of artefacts is extremely unusual in the context of world archaeology. For most periods of human history where ceramics occur, these have long been the subject of much detailed study and synthesis. As we shall see, the specific circumstances of the archaeology of the Byzantine Empire have led to this relative neglect and left this extremely rich source of information about the period largely untapped.

Although Byzantine pottery has seldom been studied, compared (for example) to Roman-period Mediterranean or medieval western European ceramics, of course, pottery is generally one of the mainstays of archaeological research. The reasons why the study of pottery is so central to archaeological research are simple and straightforward. Pottery is durable and plentiful in most periods in which it occurs and archaeologists have to use the material available to them from the past — not what they might ideally have preferred to be able to find. Because pottery survives, albeit usually as broken pieces (sherds) on most archaeological sites, almost regardless of their environmental circumstances, it is one of the most readily available archaeological sources for many historical periods. This includes the Byzantine Empire.

Moreover, in many periods of history (again, including the Byzantine period) pottery was also one of the most widely used materials in everyday life. If the archaeological significance of any object is inversely proportional to its rarity (because the more 'everyday' objects are, the more they tell us about everyday life) then pottery must rank as one of the most valuable of all archaeological sources for the Byzantine Empire. As such, it cannot remain relatively neglected and should be used to extract the maximum information about the period that it is able to provide.

To use pottery in this way it has, of course, to be dated and the place of its manufacture needs to be established. In order to help with dating, sourcing and interpretation, all pottery is first put into groups (called here 'classes') based on similarities in manufacturing techniques (such as the use of glaze) and the clay used (the 'fabric'). These classes may be further subdivided by reference to the type of decoration and the profile of the vessel, that is, the 'form' of the pot. Occasionally — more often in the case of Byzantine ceramics than is perhaps usual in pottery in general worldwide — decoration and form may correlate closely with distinct manufacturing techniques and fabrics.

Once defined in this way, each class can be designated (as here also) by a unique descriptive group name (often followed by the use of the suffix 'Ware'), for example 'Polychrome Ware' or 'Green and Brown Painted Ware'. Occasionally,

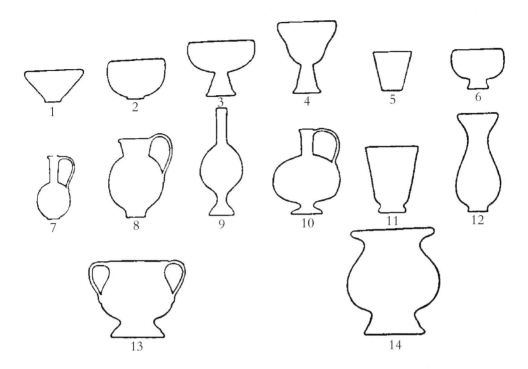

*2 Late Byzantine pottery shapes depicted in the frescos of the monasteries of Mount Athos.
1 Philotheon, Chilandari; 2 Lavra Trapeza; 3 Vatopedi, Lavra Katholikon, Lavra
Trapeza; 4 Philotheon; 5 Philotheon, Lavra Katholikon, Koutloumoussiou;
6 Xenophontos; 7 Protaton, Lavra Trapeza, Lavra Katholikon, Koutloumoussiou;
8 Chilandari; 9 Philotheon, Lavra Katholikon, Lavra Trapeza; 10 Lavra Katholikon,
Lavra Trapeza; 11 Protaton, Chilandari, Lavra Katholikon, Koutloumoussiou;
12 Lavra Katholikon; 13 Protaton; 14 Vatopedi, Lavra Trapeza.*
By David Talbot Rice, reproduced with the kind permission of the Talbot
Rice family

classes are called after the site where they were first identified or where kilns for
their manufacture were found, such as 'Zeuxippus Ware' or 'Serres Ware'. Such a
classification on the basis of technology, fabric and, in some cases, decoration and
form, enables similar pottery on different sites to be discussed together and dated
as a group, even when not found in otherwise datable contexts. Sometimes
detailed changes in specific forms permit even more precise dating, but all this
depends upon the quality of the dating evidence and the frequency with which
such changes occurred.

It is therefore important to consider (albeit briefly) exactly how pottery is
dated. When the artefacts — including pottery — found in a layer of soil during
an archaeological excavation cannot have got into the layer after the date of its

formation, then they may be considered 'sealed' in that layer. If one or more of these artefacts is independently datable (for example, if it is a coin bearing a date), then this sealed datable object provides a *terminus post quem* date for that layer, so that the layer is of the same date *or later* than the earliest possible date of the latest independently datable sealed artefact in it. That is, if a layer contains a hundred sealed ninth-century coins and only one sealed coin of AD 1000, that layer still has a *terminus post quem* of AD 1000.

Occasionally, excavated stratigraphical sequences can also be provided with a *terminus ante quem* date. Such a date is given where an overlying layer or a feature cutting it (such as a mosaic floor containing an inscription) is so certainly dated that all the layers beneath it must be the same date or earlier than that date (the opposite to a *terminus post quem* date). The absolute dating of the layer or feature providing the *terminus ante quem* date can only be provided by physically present material. For example, it cannot be derived from the extrapolation of textually known dates (such as the burning of a town) to archaeological deposits, no matter how convincing a case can be made for such a correlation.

Using such sequences of layers it is possible to assign broad dates to the pottery found in them. As most sites lack any closer dating than sequences of *terminus post quem* dated deposits, obviously such sequences only offer reliable dates for pottery when it is found on several separate sites and can be related both to *terminus post quem* and *terminus ante quem* dates. Unfortunately, at present no laboratory-based technique offers any more precise way of dating pottery than the combination of stratified sequences of coin-dated sealed deposits with rare *terminus ante quem* dates. Moreover, dates based on this method are less precise than might be possible in theory if few well-excavated stratified sequences of this sort have been fully published. This is regrettably the case for most of the Byzantine period.

Manufacturing techniques, fabric, decoration and form also provide clues as to where a pot was produced. Locating kilns or waste products discarded in manufacturing ('wasters') can further assist in identifying pottery production sites, as can studies of the mineral particles and other material ('inclusions') incorporated in the fabric of pots. These may be studied in relation to the geology of different areas, localizing the clay from which the pottery was made. Likewise, the chemical characteristics of clay can be used to 'characterize' clay sources or the minerals used in glazes, giving the same sort of results.

On this basis, pottery can usually be dated and its place of manufacture can often be located. This, in turn, enables it to be used as a source of knowledge about the past in itself and for dating archaeological layers (and from this, whole archaeological sites) in excavation and survey. Once a class has been confidently dated elsewhere, pottery of that class can be used to help assign *terminus post quem* dates to layers in excavation and to date scatters of objects found on the surface of ploughed fields during archaeological survey, or exposed through erosion, development or other non-archaeological earthmoving. Frequently, the dating of entire sequences of activity at excavated sites, or whole settlement-patterns reconstructed from survey-evidence, depends upon pottery dating.

So, pottery affords an extremely widespread and valuable source for understanding the past, both in its own right and as a means of dating sites found in archaeological excavations and surveys. But, as we have seen, pottery dating is dependent upon well-conducted and well-published stratigraphical excavations, creating a reflexive relationship between pottery dating, excavation methods and the study of other dating evidence.

It is, therefore, regrettable that Byzantine ceramics have received relatively little modern study. For pottery to be a useful source for archaeologists, it needs to be consistently identified and published. Its dating, source and geographical distribution need to be established. Byzantine pottery is often found in excavation and survey work in the Mediterranean and there is certainly much unpublished material in storage today — often the 'by-product' of studies of Classical or prehistoric sites — even outside that area. But it remains the subject of very little concerted study. The identification of Byzantine pottery is often so inconsistent in its attribution to class and use of terminology as to render comparison between even published material fraught with difficulties.

This book is intended to fulfil four main purposes. First, it attempts to draw together what we know about Byzantine pottery as a whole and discuss this as the basis of new archaeological synthesis and analysis. These allow new interpretations of the Byzantine past based on ceramic evidence that go beyond observations on the date, source and technology of the pottery discussed here. In this respect, this book is a research work, intended for professional archaeologists specializing on the Roman or Byzantine periods, the Middle East, the Mediterranean or south-east Europe, for scholars of Byzantine Studies and those working in related fields. They will find here much that is wholly new, ranging from hitherto unpublished pottery and evidence regarding its date and production, to new perspectives on Byzantine society and economy derived from looking afresh at available data. It is the only work so far published offering a synthesis of this material as a whole.

The second purpose of this work is to provide a guide to Byzantine pottery for fieldworkers and museum-cataloguers faced with ceramics they know, or suspect, to be Byzantine. These may be in museums or found during excavation or survey in the Mediterranean lands or elsewhere. Situations in which this book might be used in this way include on-site finds work during excavation, preliminary publication of excavated ceramics, and registering and archival classification of museum collections or surface-survey finds from 'fieldwalking'. In this respect, it is intended as a work of initial reference, pending specialist examination of pottery, or for use where such specialist attention is, for some reason, unlikely.[2]

To assist in consistent and swift identification in the field or museum, and to avoid burdening the text with lengthy descriptions, some of the best dated classes of pottery discussed here are described in more detail in a summary catalogue, comprising the second part of this book. Sufficient detail is given there to enable a non-specialist to identify sherds of these wares, and to provide broad dates for them in fieldwork or museum-cataloguing.

Experience shows that it is rare to encounter a group of Byzantine pottery that includes none of the classes of pottery included in the catalogue. This should, therefore, provide sufficient information to make rapid assessments in the field of the date of assemblages from excavated layers or finds collected in surface surveys. The catalogue also serves to define more closely than in any previous work the key identifying characteristics for each class and to offer a dating-system for this pottery (in several cases revised from previous work) entirely based on coin-dated excavated deposits. Similarly, identification of the possible manufacturing-centres of this pottery is based here either on the presence of kilns or wasters, or on scientific evidence for the geological origin of minerals included in the fabric.

This catalogue can, therefore, be used by specialists to provide a more closely-defined and consistent terminology for describing Byzantine pottery (especially Middle Byzantine and Late Byzantine products) than has so far been available. It also offers a more rigorous evaluation of their possible places of production than that usually found in discussions of Middle Byzantine and Late Byzantine pottery.

The third purpose of this book is to provide an introductory and up-to-date account of Byzantine pottery for university students and non-specialists, such as scholars in other fields, amateur archaeologists and visitors to the Mediterranean or to museums containing Byzantine pottery. There is no other book that may be used reliably in this way, covering the whole of Byzantine pottery.

The fourth and final purpose of this book is to encourage new interest in this internationally important, but much neglected, body of material. Hopefully, drawing attention to it and its potential in reconstructing the Byzantine past will stimulate new work by other scholars and attract the attention of students seeking postgraduate dissertation topics.

It may also be worth saying at the outset what this book is *not* intended to be. This work is obviously not an attempt at a corpus of Byzantine pottery, or at a detailed typological study enabling pottery specialists to classify or date more precisely particular forms of specific classes of Byzantine ceramics. These would both be highly desirable, but are not my intention here. This book is not even intended as an attempt at a complete archaeological, or art historical, evaluation of these wares. It is only intended to serve the purposes already stated and to explore some interesting themes illuminated by this material, as a basis for more detailed future work.

At this point, I should thank those who have helped me prepare this book. As ever my greatest thanks are to my family for their continual encouragement, help and support, and to the excellent libraries of the universities of Reading, Oxford, Cambridge and London, without whom it would have been impossible. Likewise, access to Byzantine pottery in museum and private collections — notably at The British Museum and the Victoria and Albert Museum in London — and in the field — especially in Istanbul — has been invaluable. The help of the staff of these museums has been of great assistance, in particular that of David Buckton, Chris Entwistle and Sovati Smith at The British Museum, and Reino Liefkes and Terry Bloxham at the Victoria and Albert Museum.

Judith Herrin read an early version of the text of the catalogue and made many useful comments. Hugo Blake, Veronique François, Judith Herrin, Sean Kingsley and Jodi Magness have all taken the time to discuss aspects of Byzantine pottery with me and the latter two scholars have also provided illustrations. Nergis Günsenin and Mark Jackson have also kindly sent material for inclusion here and Veronique François has given bibliographical assistance. Jane Chedzey and Anthea Harris have assisted with work on pottery in Reading and London and discussed the material with me in detail. I am also grateful for the assistance of the American School of Archaeology at Athens and the Institute of Nautical Archaeology in the USA.

In particular, I would like to thank Nicholas Talbot Rice and family for much help in regard to Byzantine ceramics and in particular for permitting his father's excellent watercolours to be reproduced here, both on the cover and in the body of the illustrations. This book is dedicated to Nicholas's father, Professor David Talbot Rice, who inaugurated the modern study of Byzantine pottery with his seminal 1930 book *Byzantine Glazed Pottery*.

1 An introduction to Byzantine pottery

Introduction: putting Byzantium in its place

The Byzantine Empire remains far less well known to most archaeologists than its Western Roman counterpart. So, it may be useful first to put the pottery discussed in this book into a broad historical context, by giving a very brief summary of the main periods of Byzantine history.

While the Western Roman Empire underwent the transition to barbarian rule and political fragmentation in the fifth century, in the eastern Mediterranean the Eastern Roman (that is, Byzantine) Empire survived largely intact as a recognizably 'Roman' polity, albeit with many internal changes and greatly fluctuating borders. This 'Roman Empire' only finally came to an end after the Ottoman capture of Constantinople in 1453. That is — in western European terms — the Byzantine Empire ended only as the Renaissance began and only about a generation before Columbus sailed to the Americas. This empire was, then, so long-

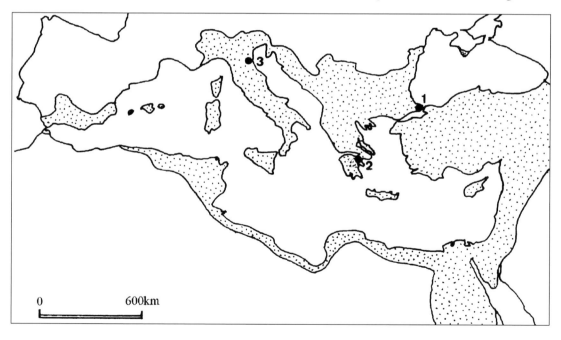

3 Map of the Early Byzantine Empire after the conquests during the reign of Justinian I c.565. 1 Constantinople; 2 Corinth; 3 Ravenna. After Buckton

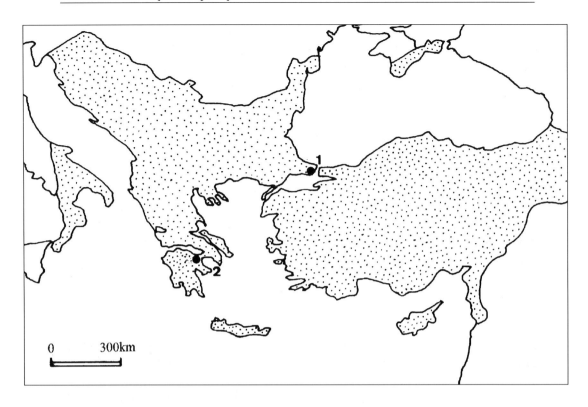

4 *Map of the Middle Byzantine Empire in 1025. 1 Constantinople; 2 Corinth.*
After Buckton

lived that it was contemporary with St Patrick and Clovis, Bede and Charlemagne, the Vikings and Alfred the Great, the Norman invasion of England and the medieval Europe of feudal chivalry and the Crusades.

The Byzantine Empire passed through three main periods in its political and cultural history. In the first period, the Early Byzantine period, the Empire retained almost every aspect of the Roman past. Large 'Roman' cities, such as Aphrodisias, Ephesus, Phillipi, Sardis and Thessaloniki flourished and sea-borne trade boomed. Cultural life retained most of the Classical heritage, alongside increasing Christianization, in a multicultural part of the Roman Empire. This phase of Byzantine history is often characterized as part of a broader world of 'Late Antiquity', perhaps stretching from the Crimea to Britain and from the Rhine to Ethiopia and the Sudan.[1]

By the early sixth century, the Byzantine Empire — under its most famous emperor, Justinian I — began an effort to re-conquer what had been the Western Roman Empire. At first this was very successful, with Italy, Sicily and North Africa all taken under Byzantine rule, but the campaign soon faltered and then started to unravel. The situation collapsed into military and economic crisis following the loss of large parts of the Empire to the Arabs and other non-Roman peoples in the seventh century, a catastrophe accentuated by widespread plague.

In the seventh and eighth centuries, the Byzantines lost effective control of most of the Balkans and lost the whole of Palestine and North Africa. Town life collapsed across large tracts of Byzantine-controlled Anatolia. Large and wealthy cities — such as Ephesus — apparently became little more than hamlets at the foot of castle-like hilltop fortresses protecting administrators and cathedrals. Religious conflict between those supporting the devotional use of religious pictures and those (the Iconoclasts) who opposed them intensified, with the imperial government adopting the Iconoclast position in the early eighth century.

Some scholars define the seventh century and the period of official Iconoclasm as a 'Dark Age'. But this is based so strongly on value-judgements about the merits of Classical culture and of the Iconoclast position that — at least from an archaeological standpoint — it is probably best to see the end of the seventh century as initiating the second main period of Byzantine history: the Middle Byzantine period. In this way, the seventh century appears as the final stage of the Early Byzantine period and the eighth century as the formative stage of Middle Byzantine Culture, in which the cultural conventions of Late Antiquity were challenged by new beliefs and values.

Through the eighth and early ninth centuries the Imperial government maintained its Iconoclast stance, in a general context of political and military difficulties for the Empire. But by 843, when Iconoclasm was officially abandoned, the Byzantine Empire was emerging from this protracted phase of recovery from its seventh-century crisis. Political and military circumstances had improved and there is evidence of renewed economic growth. Towns gradually expanded in size, although in a new 'medieval' form in which Roman public amenities had largely ceased to exist and almost the only civic buildings were now churches. The society that emerged from the ninth-century recovery was focused on the imperial court, the city of Constantinople, the Orthodox Church and the army.

Sustained military successes ensured that by the end of the ninth century imperial order was returned to large parts of the Empire in the eastern Mediterranean and Byzantine government was restored to the Balkans. The West, Palestine and North Africa were never recovered, although a Byzantine enclave lingered on in Italy. Despite major setbacks (in particular a disastrous defeat by the Seljuks at Manzikert in 1071, which led to loss of most of Anatolia) the ninth to twelfth centuries are often seen today as the 'classic age' of Byzantine civilization. Few, if any, scholars doubt that a distinctively Byzantine style of art and architecture flourished during these centuries and Byzantine culture was exported far beyond imperial borders to neighbouring peoples in eastern Europe.

The Middle Byzantine period came to an end when the Fourth Crusade captured and sacked Constantinople in 1204. Most imperial lands passed under Western (normally termed 'Latin') rule. Byzantine control lingered on in a few parts of the Empire, and in 1261 the capital and a core area around the Aegean were recaptured. A much-reduced version of the Empire survived until 1453 when Constantinople fell to the Ottoman sultan and the Empire ceased to exist.

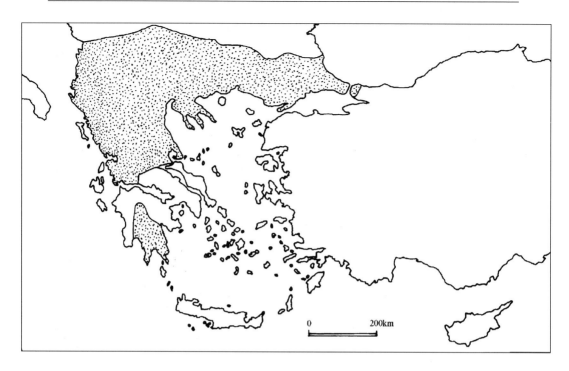

5 Map of the Late Byzantine Empire. After Haldon

It might be supposed that a thousand-year long Christian 'Roman' Empire, spanning Europe and Asia, with a capital city famous for its grandeur and playing a central role in the formation of European and Middle Eastern civilization, would have attracted much archaeological attention. But this is far from true.

The current state of Byzantine archaeology

While the archaeology of the Western Roman Empire is a well-established field, attracting a vast amount of work, the Byzantine Empire (especially after *c.*700) in general remains relatively little studied by archaeologists. Some research on Early Byzantine archaeology takes place within the remit of more wide-ranging 'Roman archaeology', but very few archaeologists anywhere in the world are employed primarily to study the Middle or Late Byzantine Empire. Few even work on these subjects at all, compared for example to Medieval western Europe.

Unlike either Roman or western medieval archaeology, Byzantine archaeology is seldom taught as a separate subject in, for example, western European or North American universities. Even compared to Islamic archaeology, it remains little represented in major research programmes undertaken by western European or North American academics.

This is not — as might be hoped — because Byzantine archaeology is a field fully covered by archaeologists based within what was once Byzantine territory. For instance, only a few professional archaeologists work wholly on the Byzantine period in Turkey and Greece, and these scholars often lack the funding and other resources to conduct large-scale research projects.

Amateur archaeology, which has a high profile role in some western European countries, is largely absent from most of south-east Europe and the Middle East. 'Archaeological societies', of the sort widely found in the UK, are almost unheard of throughout most of this zone. So, amateurs are not 'stepping into the breach' to fill in for the absence of professionals.

Indeed, Middle and Late Byzantine archaeology today is in many respects less studied than, for example, Romano-British archaeology in 1950. Many major Byzantine sites dating from *c*.700-*c*.1450 have never been excavated using modern methods. 'Open-area' stratigraphical excavation on sites of this date remains patchy throughout the former Byzantine world.

Yet, this is not to say that the Byzantine Empire in general lacks academic attention. Far from it, 'Byzantine Studies' is a well-established and lively academic discipline in the whole of Europe and the USA. But the focus of Byzantine Studies as an academic subject has been (and arguably still is) largely on the written and artistic remains of the Empire.

Historians and art historians have long examined these sources and constructed a detailed and vivid picture of society, economy and culture in an autocratic state, with a complex administrative bureaucracy and money-based market economy. They have demonstrated how Byzantine rule brought together peoples and languages from throughout the eastern Mediterranean, under what was first an officially Latin-speaking and then officially Greek-speaking government. They have examined many facets of life in an empire of towns and villages, villas and farmsteads, and churches and monasteries. They have reconstructed the beliefs and values of the people involved. Most of all they have shown the central role that the officially sponsored state Church (the Orthodox Church) played in everyday life throughout the period and outlined the intellectual and artistic cultures of the Byzantines.

Such work has provided a very valuable contribution to understanding the Byzantine Empire. However, written and artistic sources alone cannot elucidate all aspects of Byzantine life. As important as these forms of investigation are for reconstructing the Byzantine Empire, the experience of both western European medieval archaeology and of Roman archaeology demonstrates the wealth of additional information that material evidence has the potential to provide. Archaeology also has the ability to counteract the deliberate creation of self-images through writing and art, a problem that besets much text-based and art historical study of the Byzantine world.[2]

The potential afforded by Byzantine archaeology might, therefore, be supposed to be at least as great as that of Western Roman archaeology. Yet — apart perhaps from studies of church architecture, coins and seals — this potential is largely unrealized at present. Almost every subject in Byzantine archaeology requires more, and more rigorous, study and this is especially true of the period after *c*.700. Even such work that has been undertaken on Middle and Late Byzantine archaeology has frequently focused on standing structures, especially those that feature prominently in written sources, and the most elaborate works of Byzantine art. The everyday life of 'ordinary people' (the secular poor or 'middle class') after the seventh century has been almost entirely neglected. Middle and Late Byzantine domestic architecture has been largely ignored, especially outside palatial or monastic contexts.[3]

Thus, our knowledge of, for example, the development of the typical Middle Byzantine 'cross-in-square' church plan, is disproportionate to our knowledge of Middle Byzantine rural houses. This situation would be understandable if one was discussing the development of archaeology during the eighteenth and nineteenth centuries, but it has prevailed up to and including the start of the twenty-first century in many parts of what was once the Byzantine Empire.[4]

Of course, there have been notable and praiseworthy exceptions to this generalization. But on the whole, many of the most basic archaeological tasks remain to be undertaken, especially if they do not involve churches, fortifications and palaces. This focus on religious and palatial architecture (while valuable in itself) has probably impeded the further development of the field. It reflects an over-emphasis on those parts of society that feature most prominently in textual accounts of the Empire: the imperial and religious authorities and the army.

This contrasts with conventional archaeological methods and research strategies. Archaeologists elsewhere in the world generally argue that artefacts and structures relating to the everyday life of the majority of the population afford the most useful information about the past. 'Glamorous' as they may be, monasteries and palaces cannot be said to reflect daily life for most people in the Byzantine Empire, even if some churches were integrated into patterns of rural and urban living. This need to examine the everyday material culture of the majority of the population more fully brings us back to pottery.

Some initial comments on Byzantine pottery

The Byzantines used a lot of pottery. 'Fine-ware' vessels were made for table use or display and 'coarse-wares' were used for cooking and storage. Round-bottomed amphorae were used as containers for storing and transporting goods and ceramic lamps employed for lighting. The intended function of most of these pots is easily established, but ceramics could fulfil less obvious uses in the Byzantine Empire.

In particular, ceramics were used in architecture more than one might initially suppose. For example, purpose-made ceramic tubes, shaped like open-ended bottles (so as to join together in vaulting), are found in Early and Middle Byzantine Constantinopolitan buildings and in the Byzantine churches of sixth-century Ravenna in northern Italy. In addition to these purpose-made ceramic vault elements, whole amphorae were used in this way both in sixth-century Ravenna and in Middle Byzantine Constantinopolitan churches at the Pantocrator, Constantine Lips and Mangana complexes. This practice of using amphorae as vaulting elements survived into the Late Byzantine period, as at the church of Aphendiko at Mistra, probably constructed in 1310.[5]

Other ceramics had specific architectural purposes. Throughout the Byzantine period, some buildings used unglazed ceramic tiles on their floors and roofs, and elaborately decorated wall-tiles adorned the interior of a few Middle Byzantine buildings. Brick buildings were also very common from the fifth century onward, continuing Roman-period construction techniques. The flat rectilinear reddish coloured bricks of the Byzantine period closely resemble Roman examples and despite various scholarly attempts to spot chronologically significant variation in their form, there seem to be no size or shape characteristics capable of offering convincing dating evidence within the Byzantine period. Ornamental patterns were built up of this otherwise plain brickwork in the Middle and Late Byzantine periods, although the same technique was used less widely earlier, for example in the walls of the fifth-century basilican church at St John Studius in Constantinople.[6]

A distinctive type of brick production occurred in Early Byzantine Constantinople under the aegis of the imperial authorities. The bricks produced closely resemble 'normal', flat 'Roman' red brick, but they bear stamped inscriptions containing a few letters providing the date at which they were made. In a major, but still unpublished, study of these bricks, Jonathan Bardill has greatly enhanced our ability to use the information they offer to give the bricks exact dates and employ groups of stamped bricks to provide chronologies for excavated structures.

Although extremely helpful, there are limitations to the use of brick-stamps as dating evidence. Stamped bricks were stockpiled and reused, so only the latest dated bricks can offer a *terminus post quem* for a building in which they occur. Worse still, these bricks were only used in a limited range of constructions, mostly in Constantinople and nearby. This plainly restricts the utility of stamped bricks as dating evidence, except in relation to a limited range of — almost all Constantinopolitan — buildings. Even in the capital itself, it is difficult to be sure that one has access to the latest bricks from any site and these problems are aggravated by the use of stamped and unstamped bricks (which might or might not be of later date) in the same constructions.

In addition to these uses, pottery was also employed to make religious objects. The best known of these is a series of ceramic icons, of Middle Byzantine date, such as that of St Eudocia discovered in Istanbul. Also well-known are the so-called 'St Menas flasks', Early Byzantine circular pottery bottles with twin ring handles, depicting the Egyptian St Menas, or scenes related to his prestigious shrine at Abu Mina. This shrine, developed through imperial patronage, was a major focus for pilgrimage in the Early Byzantine period. Interestingly, the African

6   St Menas flask. Reproduced with the kind permission of The British Museum

dimension of St Menas was emphasized on these flasks, and camels and palm trees are frequently depicted in their moulded decoration.[7]

Moulded 'pilgrim flasks' were produced for other shrines in the Early Byzantine period. For example, handleless moulded pottery flasks were produced for pilgrims to the shrine of St John at Ephesus. Other religious objects were also produced in pottery, such as 'pilgrim tokens' — simple roundels of fired clay with a stamped design, commonly produced in association with Early Byzantine pilgrimage centres around the eastern Mediterranean.

Another class of ceramic objects with a religious purpose comprises *unguentaria* (oil-flasks). These are narrow bottles originally designed to hold sanctified vegetable oil, obtained from saints' shrines and frequently bearing stamped monograms. Although often neglected by archaeologists, they were widely used throughout the Early Byzantine eastern Mediterranean and are found at Istanbul, in the Aegean islands, Greece, Italy (including Sicily), North Africa, Spain and around the Black Sea. A (largely unpublished) series of small one-handled yellow- or green-glazed and unglazed jugs found at Istanbul may continue this vessel-type into the Middle Byzantine period.[8]

There were also pottery models. Painted ceramic model figures and animals from Early Byzantine Egypt seem to be toys, and human and animal models were added to glazed table-ware in the Middle Byzantine period as decoration, or even to convey visual jokes.

Thus, while most pottery was produced for the household or to transport goods, this was part of a wider use of ceramics in Byzantine society. Byzantines lived and worshipped in buildings partly constructed of ceramics (bricks, tiles etc.), their churches and monasteries contained pottery objects of devotion and pottery artefacts were taken away by pilgrims. In secular aspects of everyday life, ceramics also played a central role. Food often arrived in markets in pottery vessels and was processed, stored and cooked in pottery containers. Pottery was used to present food and drink at the table and this was consumed from pottery bowls, cups and plates. Ceramics were, therefore, much more central to Byzantine everyday life than to the lives of most people today, when plastic, metal and glass have replaced many of the functions it held. But what exactly is 'Byzantine pottery'?

Defining Byzantine pottery

'Byzantine pottery' is difficult to define. The Byzantine Empire was a political and institutional continuation of the Roman Empire, so when the 'Byzantine' period starts is naturally open to debate. Some scholars choose to begin the Byzantine period from the separation of the Roman Empire into two parts and the founda- tion of Constantinople as the eastern capital. Yet this leads to the position that one half of the same empire is called 'Roman' in, say, *c*.400 and the other is called 'Byzantine'. Clearly, such a terminology is unhelpful when these relate to parts of the same political entity.[9]

Others prefer a 'late' chronology, in which the Byzantine period does not start until after the so-called 'Seventh Century Transformation' when, among other things, the politics and economy of the West became more clearly separated from that of the eastern Mediterranean. After this point the Byzantines never stood a chance of re-establishing Roman rule in the West as a whole, although even in the sixth century they had recaptured Rome and Italy, along with North Africa and Sicily.

The principal problem with this 'late' start for the Byzantine period is that it leaves some of the greatest rulers, most important events and major architectural works usually considered to 'belong' to the Byzantines as 'non-Byzantine'. For example, by this token, perhaps the greatest Byzantine emperor of all — Justinian I — and the great church that he commissioned in Constantinople (Hagia Sophia) would both be non-Byzantine as they belong to the sixth century.

To most scholars of Byzantine Studies such a situation would be untenable. Applying such a rule to the archaeology of the Byzantine capital would also render the vast city walls, the famous church of Hagia Eirene (the largest surviving church building in the capital apart from Hagia Sophia), the main surviving parts of the Great Palace of the Byzantine emperors and principal extant parts of the main public space, the chariot-racing track (known as the Hippodrome), all 'non-Byzantine'. This may help to show that this approach to defining the Byzantine period is even less helpful than the first, at least from an archaeological viewpoint.

A more useful alternative may be to take the political separation and collapse of the Western Roman Empire in the early fifth century as the beginning of the Byzantine period in the East. After that time only one half of the Roman Empire was under Roman rule. This does not draw a division between the Late Roman and Byzantine periods in the fourth century, leaving half of the Empire called 'Byzantine' and half called 'Roman'. Yet it allows Justinian I, Hagia Sophia and the sixth-century Great Palace to all be 'Byzantine', not 'Late Roman' or 'Late Antique'.

The end of the Byzantine period is more easily defined. The city of Constantinople fell to the forces of sultan Mohammed 'the Conqueror' in May 1453. Although a 'Post-Byzantine' state lingered on for a while in the Black Sea coast of what is today northern Turkey, thereafter there was no attempt to revive the Byzantine Empire. The last area of what had been the Roman Empire still under 'Roman' rule had passed under the control of another government. A 'Post-Byzantine' culture survived, but this was now disengaged from any existing political unit.[10]

Having defined 'Byzantine' chronologically as from the early fifth to mid-fifteenth centuries, next we need to address the geographical scope of this term. Obviously, any state that survives for a thousand years is unlikely to have static boundaries throughout that time, and this is especially true of the fluctuating borders of the Byzantine Empire. In the sixth century, the Byzantines ruled territory in Italy, Sicily, Spain, North Africa, the Balkans, the whole of Anatolia and virtually the entire eastern Mediterranean coastlands. In the 1450s only

Constantinople and its hinterland and a few patches of the Aegean coastlands were under Byzantine control. Nor was this a consistent and gradual decline, the Byzantines gained and lost territory — not necessarily the same land — throughout their history.

While some areas, such as parts of Greece and the western coast of Anatolia, remained Byzantine through most of the period from the fifth to the twelfth centuries, other areas were only periodically under Byzantine control. The short-lived 'Latin Empire' in the eastern Mediterranean further complicates the geopolitical situation. In the 1260s the Byzantines regained the core of their former territory, but for half the thirteenth century almost all the formerly Byzantine lands were under western European rule.[11]

These shifts in political control and cultural dominance obviously cause problems for anyone studying Byzantine material culture. Material things seldom come with cultural 'labels' attached and one has to assign them to political and cultural groups known from historical sources, or decide to disregard those historically-known groups and treat the material culture as an entirely separate thing from non-material identity and culture. If we aim to use material culture to study a specific empire or 'civilization', then we have no alternative but to adopt the former approach, allowing for the theoretical and methodological difficulties implicit in it.

In this book, 'Byzantine pottery' is defined as pottery that was either certainly or probably manufactured within the boundaries of the Byzantine Empire as they were at the date of its manufacture, on the basis of those grounds for identifying its place of manufacture stated in the preface. This excludes all the Chinese, Islamic and Western products found on Byzantine sites or in areas once part of the Byzantine Empire, but includes imitations of non-Byzantine products by potters located within Byzantine territory. In periods where the Empire fragmented and former Byzantine lands were ruled by independent 'Byzantine' governments, or had 'Byzantine' populations who continued to manufacture classes of pottery that were first introduced under Byzantine rule, we may allow their pottery also to be called 'Byzantine'. Non-Byzantine ceramics will be mentioned in the text only where relevant to pottery-use in the Byzantine Empire or to Byzantine ceramic technology or typology. This offers a definition of Byzantine pottery analogous to that used to designate 'Roman pottery', usually understood as 'pottery manufactured in the Roman Empire'.

Obviously, one can never show that every such pot was certainly manufactured by 'a Byzantine' rather than anyone else, but it is equally unlikely that all of what is generally referred to as 'Roman pottery' was the work of Roman citizens. So this definition will serve as a useful basis for identifying 'Byzantine pottery' here, rather than appeal to vague notions of a Byzantine ceramic 'tradition' or simply the study of pottery found within what was the Byzantine Empire.

The study of Byzantine ceramics

Although, as mentioned in the preface, this is the first book on Byzantine pottery as whole, Byzantine ceramics have been academically studied since the nineteenth century. In the nineteenth and early twentieth centuries this study — by pioneering scholars such as Wallis, Dawkins, Droop, Ebersolt and Mamboury — was both intermittent and largely focused on single excavations or museum collections, at most on single towns. For instance, when the famous Constantinopolitan Mangana monastic complex was excavated, the pottery discovered there was published in detail in the final excavation report. But this was not followed by any synthetic study of Byzantine pottery in the City or at other monasteries, building on the dating evidence that this material could have provided.[12]

In general, except where discussing single sites, most nineteenth- and early twentieth-century work on Byzantine pottery was not based on the study of excavated deposits, but on art-historical criteria alone. Needless to say, this did not usually produce reliable dates for the pottery concerned and the chronology and nature of the material remained only vaguely understood into the 1920s, when new excavations at Istanbul produced new and more reliably-dated groups of pottery from stratified deposits.

This prompted the turning point in the study of Byzantine pottery: David Talbot Rice's classic book *Byzantine Glazed Pottery*. Published in 1930, Talbot Rice's book remained the only one-volume, extensively illustrated, overview of Byzantine glazed ceramics in general up until the end of the twentieth century. In his study, Talbot Rice, who had worked on the finds from the British excavations at the Hippodrome in Istanbul, set out a classification and approximate dating for Middle and Late Byzantine glazed fine-wares, which remains the foundation for all subsequent work.[13]

Another British archaeologist, R.B.K. Stevenson, also made a notable contribution to Byzantine pottery studies by working on finds from the Great Palace of Byzantine Constantinople. He realized that the large quantities of well-stratified pottery found in close association with datable coins during the 1930s excavations (the excavations currently displayed in the Mosaic Museum at Istanbul) enable the construction of a clear-cut chronology for the pottery at the site and, by implication, for the whole Byzantine capital. This development was consolidated, when Talbot Rice succeeded Stevenson in this role, carrying his work into the 1950s. This combined the achievements of the two outstanding mid-twentieth-century scholars in this field into a single project, and laid the foundation for all subsequent studies of Middle and Late Byzantine pottery.[14]

While central to the later development of Byzantine pottery studies, this work was not in isolation. American archaeologists, in particular, were also making important contributions to Byzantine pottery studies in the 1930s-50s. Foremost among these is the work of Alison Frantz at Athens and especially Charles Morgan at Corinth. These scholars began — like Talbot Rice and Stevenson at Istanbul —

to use coin-dating and stratigraphy to date Byzantine pottery. These contributions laid a firm basis for later Byzantine pottery studies in Greece, analogous to that established slightly earlier in Istanbul.[15]

By 1960, an outline chronology for Middle and Late Byzantine pottery was available. Nevertheless, much of this chronology still rested on art-historical arguments about the dating of decorative motifs, rather than coin-dated stratified deposits. Consequently, many chronological uncertainties and imprecisions of classification were apparent and the relevance of this chronology outside Istanbul and Greece was uncertain.

During the 1960s-90s, this outline classification and chronology was greatly elaborated by English-speaking scholars. Especially important studies were undertaken by: Pamela Armstrong, Eunice Dauterman Maguire, Judith Herrin, Jodi Magness, Henry Maguire, Arthur Megaw, Guy Sanders, Theodora Stillwell-Mackay, Joanita Vroom, Pamela Watson and Caroline Williams. Greek and Turkish archaeologists also made a notable contribution to this field during these decades, especially Charalambos Bakirtzis and Demetra Papanikola-Bakirtzi in Greece and Nergis Günsenin in Turkey. Other western European scholars, in particular Veronique François, Jean-Pierre Sodini, Jean-Michel Spieser, and Urs Peschlow also had a very important role in furthering the study of this material during the last decades of the twentieth century.[16]

Nonetheless, the foremost contribution to the understanding of Byzantine pottery in the second half of the twentieth century was by John Hayes. Hayes's magisterial book *Late Roman Pottery* provided a framework for the modern study of the Early Byzantine fine-wares. This placed Early Byzantine pottery classification and chronology — which had long benefited from links with the far more developed area of Roman pottery studies — on a sound archaeological footing. In particular, Hayes demonstrated that the main Early Byzantine fine-wares might be coin-dated to within a few decades — using well-sealed stratigraphically excavated deposits throughout the Mediterranean and beyond. This gave fifth- to seventh-century fine-wares the same level of chronological precision as well-dated Roman-period pottery and this is still the best-dated group of Byzantine pottery.

Hayes followed this fundamental work on Early Byzantine pottery with an outstanding study of the ceramics from Saraçhane excavation in Istanbul, offering a similar rigour to Middle Byzantine pottery from Constantinople. Hayes has also pioneered the recognition of the earliest Byzantine glazed wares, crucial for the origins of Middle Byzantine fine-wares, and made major contributions to the study of Byzantine amphorae and coarse-wares in his work at Saraçhane and elsewhere.[17]

During the 1960s-90s also, important work by David Peacock and David Williams on Early Byzantine amphorae established amphora chronologies on as firm a footing as their fine-ware counterparts. Their use of laboratory-based analysis to study this material greatly clarified patterns of manufacture and distribution and this was further assisted in the last quarter of the twentieth century by detailed examinations of Byzantine amphorae in North Africa and western Europe.

Particularly important studies of Byzantine amphorae in these areas were under-taken by Paul Arthur, Maurice Bonifay, Ewan Campbell, Jean-Yves Empereur, Simon Keay, Marcel Picon, Paul Reynolds and, especially, John Riley.[18]

The work of these scholars has led to the study of Early Byzantine fine-wares and amphorae reaching a state of typological and chronological clarity far above that of later Byzantine pottery and equivalent to that of first- to fourth-century AD Roman pottery. However, the study of Middle and Late Byzantine wares still lags far behind these, and most Early Byzantine coarse-wares still lack detailed chronologies, despite exemplary studies such as that by Caroline Williams.[19]

Important work has also taken place on related material outside what was the Byzantine Empire. The clearest example is in Italy, where studies of medieval Italian pottery in the latter decades of the twentieth century clarified the non-Byzantine character of Proto-Maiolica Ware, 'Ramina Manganese Rosso' ('RMR') Ware and so-called 'Roulette Ware'. The widespread use of these Italian fine-wares on Late Byzantine sites and in the zones of the former Byzantine Empire ruled by Westerners during the Latin Empire of 1204-61, creates a close link between the chronology of medieval Italian and Late Byzantine ceramics. Thus, the clarification of the chronology of medieval Italian pottery, such as the dating of 'Grid Iron' and 'Grid Iron Variant' Proto-Maiolica and 'Ramina Manganese Rosso' pottery to *c.*1250-1350, has major implications for the chronology of Late Byzantine pottery and Byzantine sites as a whole.[20]

A link between Byzantine and Italian pottery studies also comes from the inclusion of Byzantine ceramics in the walls of Italian churches as *bacini* (display plates) and Italian ceramics in the walls of Byzantine churches. Similarly, studies of Crusader sites in Palestine and Cyprus have also improved understanding of related pottery produced there, such as so-called 'St Symeon Ware' and the Cypriot series of sgraffito ware bowls.[21]

Another major development in the last decades of the twentieth century was the growth of laboratory-based analyses of Byzantine and related pottery. These used the minerals incorporated in the clay or glaze of pottery to locate its source, or employed chemical or other laboratory-based methods to examine the technology of these ceramics. Studies of this sort have been underway at many centres, such as at Dumbarton Oaks in Washington DC, at the University of Illinois, at Oxford University, the University of Southampton and at the University of Reading. Some of the results of the latter study are published, in brief, for the first time in this book.[22]

Studies of this sort are especially important because few Byzantine pottery kilns or potters workshops have been excavated, although all Byzantine pottery was probably produced in purpose-built kilns. In most cases, 'wasters' (unwanted products discarded during production) give the clearest indication of the location of kilns. Wasters are unlikely to have travelled far, usually being discarded near places of manufacture. They provide an indication — but not certain proof — of manufacture in a particular locality. Plainly, the more 'waster' material the more likely it is that a given site was used for pottery manufacture, or for the dumping of pottery-manufacturing by-products from a nearby kiln. Thus, wasters provide good enough evidence to permit localization to a given city or general area, but they cannot afford the same degree of confidence as an excavated kiln site about where and how pottery was manufactured.

In order to examine Byzantine pottery in more detail, it is convenient to discuss the coarse-wares and fine-wares separately and, for reasons that will become clear, to begin with the coarse-wares. These show a remarkable continuity over a thousand years and indicate how conservatism can operate in the context of widespread pottery production and much innovation in other aspects of contemporary life and art.

2 Byzantine coarse-wares: 1000 years of continuity in pottery production?

Introduction

The material included in this chapter is defined partly by exclusion from the category of fine-wares, partly by distinctive characteristics. Coarse-wares were by far the commonest Byzantine pottery, but remain by far the least studied. Coarse-wares occur on every Byzantine settlement site — they were even found at the Great Palace of the Byzantine emperors at Constantinople. They were mostly produced and marketed very locally, probably partly by specialist potters catering for the immediate needs of local communities.

Byzantine coarse-wares require detailed area-by-area, region-by-region, investigation, but this has only just begun. So any account of this pottery at present has

7 *Early Byzantine cooking pot from the shipwreck at Yassı Ada II.* Courtesy of the Institute of Nautical Archaeology

to be somewhat 'impressionistic'. This will be the case for the foreseeable future, unless a great amount more work on these wares is undertaken and they are afforded far more time and effort by archaeologists working in the regions where they are most commonly found. Despite this, a general description of such pottery is already possible.

Early Byzantine coarse-wares

Early Byzantine 'coarse-wares' include a wide range of shapes: cooking pots, bowls, domed or saucer-shaped lids, *mortaria* (grinding bowls for preparing food), jars, jugs, cups, candlesticks, flasks, lamps, amphorae and others. Some of these shapes were manufactured in the same fabrics, but without the same finish, as Early Byzantine fine-wares, but other coarse-wares manufactured in fabrics containing more, and larger, mineral inclusions. The surfaces of these coarse-wares were usually plain, but sometimes slipped, burnished, polished or decorated with incised wavy, horizontal or slanting lines. They frequently have small handles and/or lids with handles and sometimes have other functional additions, such as integral strainers.[1]

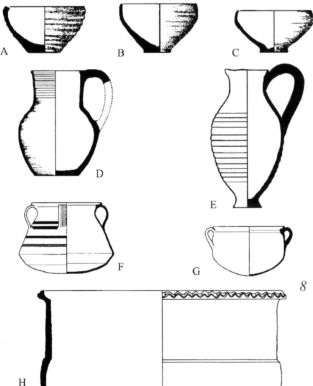

8 *Examples of forms of Early Byzantine coarse-wares. A–D Sardis; E-G Emporio; H Anemurium ('Piecrust-Rim Ware'). After* Crawford, Boardman et al. and Williams

Most cooking pots were hemispherical or globular in shape, often with ribbed external surfaces, presumably to improve grip. A distinctive form of cooking pot was 'frying pan'-shaped, comprising a shallow circular bowl with a slightly curved base and a single long handle. This shape of vessel had a very long life in the Byzantine Empire and became particularly common later in the Byzantine period, but it was produced from the start and occurs in distinctive Early Byzantine fabrics.

Textual evidence and later analogy suggests that this 'frying pan' shape was probably, in fact, used for frying food in olive oil, for parching dry foods, or making something like an omelette. So the term 'frying pan' may justifiably be applied to vessels of this shape, while not indicating that this was their exclusive function. The pottery versions existed alongside metal examples and may have been used in conjunction with a wooden spatula, much like a modern frying pan.

A common repertoire of basic coarse-ware shapes is found throughout the Early Byzantine world. For example, common sixth-century shapes include squat jars and jugs, often with a concave base with central knob. Globular cooking pots, usually with one or two small handles attached at the rim and shoulder, were especially common. These were produced throughout the Early Byzantine Empire, for example in Palestine, Egypt and Greece. Decorative techniques were also shared among the coarse-ware pottery of Early Byzantine communities. Rouletting, ribbing and incised or combed decoration were especially common. For example, these decorative techniques are evidenced on local red-pale brown jugs from Kellia in Egypt, cream-buff jugs produced at Abu Mina, also in Egypt, and on local, often red-slipped, jugs at Athens. Some of the latter are also partly burnished, as are some local products in Anatolia and Palestine. Pinched decoration is found both in Egypt, for example at Kellia, and Anatolia as at Anemurium, where it was used to manufacture the distinctive local 'Piecrust Rim Ware', characterized by its undulating finger-moulded rims.

Not withstanding this, regional forms are clearly visible among Early Byzantine coarse-wares. For example, in Egypt and Palestine some vessels had internal strainers (perhaps to prevent insects reaching the contents) and small spouts on the shoulder of the vessel. Even the external ribbing found on cooking pots may exhibit regional characteristics, for example there is a tendency for wavy, rather than horizontal, lines in the Aegean area. Likewise, deeper pots may have been used in Anatolia and the Aegean than elsewhere in the Empire.[2]

Usually, unglazed coarse-wares were produced locally and, therefore, a very wide range of fabrics exists. For example, in the well-excavated fifth- to seventh-century shops at Sardis, 75 per cent of the pottery consisted of locally produced coarse micaceous wares, and another 20 per cent of a coarse local gritty reduced black fabric.

At Constantinople the typical local coarse-ware was what can be termed Constantinopolitan Greyware. The Early Byzantine variant of this class (Hayes Saraçhane wares 1 and 3) — mainly used for cooking pots — is a light or mid-grey to grey-brown fabric with limestone, sand and mica inclusions. These become coarser and harder-fired during the course of the fifth and sixth centuries. In the centre of the southern Anatolian coast, at Anemurium, everted rimmed cooking pots were produced in a red, brown or orange-red micaceous and limestone-gritted fabric. These have one or two strap-handles joining at the body and at, or immediately below, the rim.[3]

Likewise, Sagalassos in southern Anatolia also produced its own coarse-wares. The principal fabric (Sagalassos Fabric 1) was identical to that used for Sagalassos Red-Slip Ware (discussed in the following chapter), but used partially slipped and unslipped for storage vessels and jugs. The second local variety (Sagalassos Fabric 2), which came into use from the fourth century onward, comprises a hard reddish-yellow fabric, usually unslipped and with many inclusions. Later, cooking pots were increasingly manufactured in a rough, but hard, yellowish-red fabric (Sagalassos Fabric 4) with white and red inclusions (and sometimes yellow and shiny black inclusions also), which became very common in the seventh century.[4]

It was not only Anatolian towns that produced their own coarse-wares, rural sites also manufactured most of their own pottery. At Oludeniz, further south in western Anatolia, cooking pots, vessel-lids and *stamnia* (flat-bottomed but otherwise 'amphora-like' jars) decorated with notched and wavy line incisions were produced in a local orange-buff, pink-buff or grey-buff fabric. In the Aegean islands we can see distinctive products, for example, on Chios. There, Early Byzantine coarse-wares (as found at Emporio) comprise both one- and two-handled jugs, mugs, jars, plates and round-based two-handled cooking pots in a wide range of (sometimes micaceous) gritty buff-grey-pink-red fabrics. A distinctive local coarse-ware 'industry' existed on Cyprus, which even managed to export this pottery, for example to Anemurium. Cypriot coarse-wares include cooking pots in a very hard-fired and very gritty, but only slightly micaceous, orange-red fabric with a great number of limestone inclusions, fired grey or reddish-grey on its exterior.[5]

The example of Cyprus shows that the distribution of coarse-wares was not always completely localized. Several fabrics were widely traded, such as coarse-ware products of the North African potteries also manufacturing African Red-Slip Ware in similar fabrics. Much of this trade was with adjacent regions, as might be expected, but not wholly. For example, Anemurium in southern Anatolia also received some of its imported cooking pots from Palestine and Constantinopolitan Greyware was exported as far as Carthage and Rome. Aegean and Palestinian coarse-wares have been recognized in Italy, Gaul, Spain and North Africa, albeit in small numbers. African coarse-wares have even been reported from the fifth- and sixth-century settlement at Tintagel in south-west Britain.[6]

Work by Jodi Magness in Palestine provides an exemplary study of one of these regional groups. Four principal classes of local Early Byzantine coarse-ware vessels can be recognized. Rouletted Bowls — thick-walled bowls with ring bases — were manufactured (probably close to Jerusalem, where they are common) in an orange/orange-brown fabric, with a grey core and a red, purple or brown slip. Such

9 *Early Byzantine Rouletted Bowls from modern Israel.* Reproduced with the kind permission of Jodi Magness

bowls are usually, although not always, decorated with external rouletting, hence the name. Rilled-Rim Basins and Arched Rim-Basins (both deep bowls) were produced in a similar light orange-brown/brown hard-fired fabric. Rilled-Rim Basins had vertical ledged rims externally rilled but without additional decoration, while Arched-Rim Basins have a characteristic everted rim and external combing, although this was never universal. Similar pottery was produced in what is today Jordan in the Late Roman period into the fifth century and perhaps later. 'Fine Byzantine Ware' comprises bowls, jars, cups and jugs in a thin hard-fired light brown, light orange or light orange-brown fabric. The exterior of these vessels was decorated with burnished bands, and incised decoration, often in the form of wavy lines or diagonals. The classes were all in use in the fifth and sixth centuries, but Rouletted Bowls may have passed from use in the fifth century and 'Fine Byzantine Ware' may begin in the sixth and was produced into the tenth century.[7]

10 *Early Byzantine Arched-Rim Basins from modern Israel.* Reproduced with the kind permission of Jodi Magness

11 Early Byzantine Fine Byzantine Ware from modern Israel. Reproduced with the kind permission of Jodi Magness

Palestine was not the only area with well-produced and decorated coarse-wares. For example, an Anatolian equivalent of 'Fine Byzantine Ware' is arguably 'Spiral Burnished Ware'. This is found only in Anatolia and has a micaceous pink-brown hard fabric with small lime inclusions. It is red slipped with a glossy finish on some examples, although the interior is always matt. On the exterior, interior and base, concentric lines of darker red result from the distinctive spiral burnishing. Unlike 'Fine Byzantine Ware', and perhaps in emulation of the red-slipped fine-wares, Spiral Burnished Ware was sometimes stamped with geometric motifs. This may suggest that these high-quality local wares were trying to emulate — or even compete with — the extensively traded fine-wares.

Despite this, Early Byzantine coarse-wares almost always bear a close relation to local Late Roman pottery. For example, the thin-walled cooking pots with small handles that were made into the seventh century at the Dhiorios kiln in Cyprus are reminiscent of Roman pottery. Elsewhere, they directly continued Roman provincial pottery: production of Rilled-Rim and Arched-Rim basins actually began in the third century. In general, there is no reason to doubt that these similarities represent the direct continuity of Roman coarse-ware pottery traditions throughout the Early Byzantine period.[8]

Another case of continuity across the fourth and fifth centuries is the manufacture of *mortaria*. Evidence from Anemurium suggests that stamped North

12 Early Byzantine amphorae from Yassı Ada II. Courtesy of the Institute of
Nautical Archaeology

Syrian *mortaria*, as manufactured at Ras el-Basit and with Greek stamps, were in
use into the sixth century. These are widely distributed around the eastern
Mediterranean, attesting the widespread use of such vessels.[9]

This continuity of production may also be seen in relation to both amphorae
and lamps. Amphorae are transport jars, with closed forms and rounded bases.
The standard amphora was called in the Early Byzantine period the *kouphon* and
later the *megarikon* (small vessels of similar form being termed *lagena*). These were
the main means of transporting commodities in the Early Byzantine period, and
many shipwrecks of this date show cargoes stored mainly in amphorae in their
holds. Amphorae had a long heritage in the Roman world and continued in
production beyond the frontiers of the Byzantine Empire through the Early
Byzantine period and afterwards.[10]

Early Byzantine amphorae mostly represent the direct continuation of Late
Roman types. That is, most fifth- to seventh-century Byzantine amphorae are the
products of 'industries' established prior to 400, often in the fourth century. The
principal types of Early Byzantine amphorae were widely traded and could be used
for a wide range of purposes, although most usually contained one of two main
products: wine or olive oil. Unsurprisingly, therefore, the production centres of

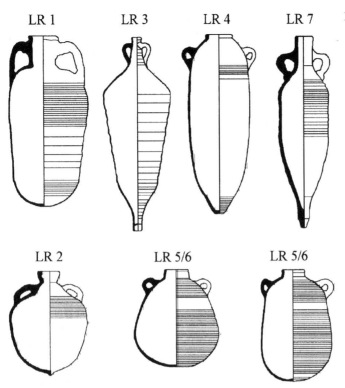

LR 1   LR 3   LR 4   LR 7

13 The main classes of Early Byzantine amphora. After Riley and Peacock and Williams

LR 2   LR 5/6   LR 5/6

amphorae tend to reflect the oil- and wine-producing areas of the Empire.

Most widely distributed Early Byzantine amphorae were produced in the eastern Mediterranean coastlands. They are usually buff-coloured, although one class is red-brown, and have either tubular or globular bodies. Handles are generally simple loops to the body or neck or — less frequently — ring-handles on the body-sides. Almost all Early Byzantine amphorae have external rilling, combing or tegulation (a tile-like effect) and most have a well-defined neck, although these features are not universal. They are extremely similar in general appearance to Roman amphorae and might be easily mistaken for them at first sight.

Seven main classes of amphora were commonly used in the Byzantine Empire. The most typologically complicated class is that of 'North African amphorae'. These are large cylindrical amphorae, with D-shaped or ring handles attached to a short neck and shoulder. The base is spiked and the exterior of the vessel is tegulated, although a few of the very wide range of specific forms have no external decoration. Not all North African amphorae were produced under Byzantine (rather than, for example, Vandal) rule, but amphorae of this class were widely available in the East even when North Africa was outside the Empire.

Three important classes of amphora were produced in the north of the eastern Mediterranean. 'LR1' was probably primarily produced in the Antioch area, perhaps to carry olive oil from Syria, but was also manufactured in Cyprus and possibly elsewhere. LR1 has a hard, sandy pink-cream or orange fabric with many limestone inclusions and a globular body with 'teacup' handles attached to the high neck and pronounced shoulder. The exterior is heavily ribbed, sometimes with Greek letters in red paint on the shoulder. It was widely traded, for example in Constantinople, Anatolia, the Aegean, the Balkans, Greece, North Africa and Palestine, although it is found in such quantities in Egypt that it is possible that it carried goods targeted at the Egyptian market.

'LR2' was probably produced in the Argolid of Greece and on the Aegean island of Chios, the latter famous in Late Antiquity for its wine. It may have carried both oil and wine and has a particularly widespread distribution, extending to Britain, Gaul and Italy in the West and across the Byzantine Empire. LR2 was produced in a hard, light, buff-red fabric with limestone inclusions and some mica, and its globular body has a characteristic band of (sometimes wavy) ribbing, with D-shaped handles. Uniquely among these amphorae, it was produced with matching pottery lids.

'LR3' is associated with the wine-producing area of western Anatolia and was perhaps manufactured near Sardis. It has a hard, very micaceous, dark to mid-red-brown fabric and a tapering body covered externally in broad ridges, and was also widely traded in both the Byzantine eastern Mediterranean and the West.

There were also major centres of amphora-production in Palestine and Egypt. The 'LR4' or 'Gaza' amphora seems to have been associated with the famous wines produced in the Gaza area of Palestine. LR4 amphorae have a hard, sandy, brown fabric (although the core is sometimes greyish) with limestone inclusions. Their long cylindrical narrow body carries narrow zones of ridging, and small upward turned D-shaped handles are attached to the body on the shoulder.

The 'LR5/6' or 'Palestinian' amphora was manufactured in two distinct fabrics (one buff-orange and the other grey with a red core) and has a characteristic 'bag-shaped' profile with a partly ribbed exterior. Small D-shaped handles are attached to the shoulder where this is ribbed and to the rim, and sometimes white painted decoration is found on the exterior. They were the main transport container for Palestinian wine in this period and widely distributed both in the West and throughout the Byzantine Empire.

The 'LR7' or 'Egyptian' amphora was produced in hard, sandy, light red-buff fabrics with a distinctive external greenish-cream slip. LR7 amphorae have bands of tegulation around the pear-shaped exterior and distinctive 'upside-down teacup' handles attached at rim and on neck. These seem to have been another standard regional transport vessel, serving the same role for Egypt as did LR5/6 in Palestine, where they were manufactured in the Nile Valley and perhaps elsewhere.

The association of each amphora class with a distinct region suggests that Early Byzantine consumers may have believed that they were able to discern the origin of an amphora and its contents from its appearance alone, perhaps even using these as the equivalent of modern 'produce of . . .' labels on fruit and vegetables. However, if so they may have been mistaken. Imitations of these amphora classes were produced outside the areas with which they are most strongly associated. For example, despite its association with Gaza, LR4 was also

14 Early Byzantine amphora from the shipwreck at Yassı Ada II. Courtesy of the Institute of Nautical Archaeology

produced in Egypt, where kilns for this have been found near Alexandria. One wonders if the production of 'Gaza' amphorae in Egypt was a deliberate attempt to deceive, or whether the produce being carried was in some way suitably 'Gazan', such as wine from vines originating in the Gaza area.

Amphorae production continued throughout the Early Byzantine period, in most cases with only subtle typological change. Considerable variation existed within each class at any one time in the lesser details of individual amphorae. Usually it is possible only to assign these vessels to a broad fifth- to seventh-century date-range, rather than to offer more chronological precision on the basis of form. This alone should assure us of the continuity of the Roman tradition of amphora-manufacture throughout these centuries.

Another long-lived form of ceramic production was the manufacture of lamps. Early Byzantine lamps derive directly from Late Roman predecessors and were closed vessels with one small handle or without a handle. They have one or more openings for pouring in the olive oil used as fuel and for inserting a wick. Ceramic lamps were produced throughout the Early Byzantine Empire and a large amount of standardization was afforded by the use of stone or plaster moulds. Lamps frequently bore moulded decoration or even inscriptions, both increasingly of a Christian religious character after the fifth century. Pottery lamps were widely traded and copied, but work has defined a number of distinctive regional classes and fabrics, of which the most common by far are Anatolian ('Asia Minor') products, lamps from Greece and, especially, North African lamps.[11]

'Asia Minor' lamps were produced in a fine matt red or brown slipped orange- or red-brown micaceous fabric, probably at or near Ephesus, in the fifth to seventh centuries. These often have a 'fish-tail' design of grooves by the solid handle, a flattish circular or occasionally oval shape, a broad raised base-ring and clay globules applied to the top to create a distinctive 'pimply' effect. Similar lamps, in a superficially similar fabric, were produced at Sardis, in (sometimes unslipped) orange, red or brown very micaceous clay. Cnidus may have been another centre of lamp production in the fifth and sixth centuries, employing a coarser micaceous orange, red or light brown fabric, sometimes slipped bright orange.

The micaceous fabrics of these Anatolian products contrast with those of other regions. Beginning in the fourth century, North African pottery lamps soon became the most widely used of all. North African lamps were manufactured in the 'brick red' fabric used for African Red Slip Ware and are divisible into two main types, as defined by John Hayes.

The first (Hayes I) has a keyhole-shaped top with sloping edges and a solid handle. Hayes II, the second type, has a knob-like handle and stamped decora-

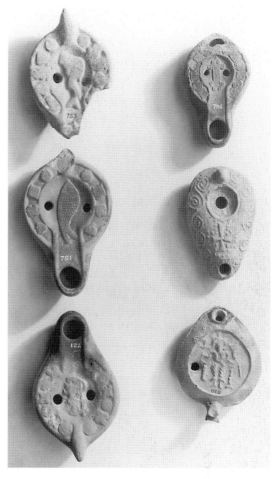

15 Early Byzantine pottery lamps.
Reproduced with the kind permission of The British Museum

tion on the top with a raised band at the edges. These lamps were widely exported, even to areas that manufactured lamps themselves. They were often copied in local fabrics, as at Corinth where imitations in a hard buff or red-brown fabric are found.

Both Athenian and Corinthian lamp production continued from the Late Roman period, with glazed products curiously dating largely from the fourth century and earlier. Although fifth-century glazed lamps were probably produced in Athens, apart from this, Early Byzantine lamps in Greece are generally unglazed. One distinctive chronological feature is the use of Christian symbols in the decoration of 'Greek' lamps from the fifth century onward. Corinthian lamp manufacture seems to have ceased in the late sixth century but Athenian production probably lasted into the eighth century.

16 Mould for African Red Slip Ware pottery lamp. Reproduced with the kind permission of The British Museum

Corinthian lamp manufacture specialized in copying imported lamps in a hard and dark red-brown or, less often, pale buff fabric, often with limestone inclusions. During the sixth century, Athenian lamps also tended to copy imported examples or produce simpler local versions, probably indicating declining local technical standards. Another copying centre was probably at Argos, where a mould for this purpose has been found.

This merely gives a sample of the more widely traded regional classes. There were, of course, other manufacturers of similar lamps outside these areas, as in Thrace, Egypt, Palestine and Constantinople itself. For example, oval lamps, often carinated, with stubby handles and sometimes carrying religious inscriptions in Greek, characterize Early Byzantine production in Palestine, Syria, Cyprus and Egypt. A rare variant is multi-wick lamps, where a circular tube was filled with oil lighting several adjacent wicks each with a separate hole in its upper surface. This rare type of lamp, intended for suspension from the ceiling, was probably for church use.

That is, Early Byzantines cooked with, ate from and stored their food in pottery vessels almost identical to that used in the Late Roman period. Their buildings were also constructed of bricks and tiles that 'looked Roman' and lit with lamps equally similar to their Late Roman antecedents. Commodities were transported in vessels that it would — at first sight — usually be difficult to distinguish from those of the fourth century. In all these respects, ceramics attest just how 'Late Roman' the material culture of Early Byzantine everyday life really was.

This is not especially surprising, as few scholars have doubted that a high degree of cultural and economic continuity existed between the Late Roman and Early Byzantine periods in the eastern Mediterranean. What is more surprising is to find that this general continuity continues in many aspects of coarse-ware production into the Middle Byzantine period.

Middle Byzantine coarse-wares

The seventh century was in many ways a period of profound change for the Byzantine Empire. But this change is not very visible in terms of coarse-ware pottery. Overall, Middle Byzantine coarse-wares continue local production in a narrow range of Late Roman shapes with little trace of major change in the vessels used. This is evidenced, for example, by Middle Byzantine coarse-wares found at Sardis, Ephesus, Pergamon, Thessaloniki and Athens. Middle Byzantine coarse-ware reproduced the local Early Byzantine repertoire including jugs, jars, and cooking pots with one, two or no handles. Another distinctive shape was a two-handled flask, resembling earlier St Menas flasks.[12]

Like their Early Byzantine counterparts too, Middle Byzantine cooking pots often had ridges on the exterior and were sometimes provided with lids. Their bases were rounded or flat, usually the former, and their handles usually looped upward like modern teacup handles, although inverted U-shaped handles are also known. There seems to be an association between cooking pots with one handle and flat bases and two-handled and round bottomed cooking vessels. This is also reflected in size differences, with the one-handled pots being smaller.

17 Examples of forms of Middle Byzantine coarse-wares. A Corinth; B, C and E Argos; D Serçe Limani; F Thassos. After Bakirtzis and Sanders

Cooking pots without handles are usually the smallest vessels; perhaps tongs were used to handle them.

Just as these forms of cooking vessels continued to resemble those of the Early Byzantine, at least in general terms, so too did their decoration. The most common variety of decoration remained bands of horizontal or wavy lines on the exterior, or bands of pinched decoration applied as vertical or horizontal strips on the exterior of the body. Additional decoration — more rarely found — includes multiple ridges near the mouth of the vessel and thin bands of relief decoration, perhaps rendering a 'skeuomorph' of rope (used on vessels for carrying?) around the body and in vertical lines to immediately below the rim.

Like cooking-pots, Middle Byzantine coarse-ware jars also resemble Roman-period vessels, with oval or globular bodes, flat bases and everted rims. Decoration is limited to bands of straight and wavy lines on the exterior, although sometimes mica was added to the slip to give this a metallic sheen, as in the case of two-handled jars from Pergamon. The largest jars, globular *pithoi*, were set into the ground to hold water, grain or other goods.

Jugs were also produced which resemble those of the Early Byzantine period. These include vessels with round, pinched and trefoil lips, those with long slender necks and thicker shorter necks, and those with globular or near-spherical bodies. 'Teacup' and simple loop handles are found on these jugs and decoration is normally less common than on jars, although bands of rilling or wavy and zig-zag lines occur. However, some highly-decorated jugs are known, as at Ephesus, with scalloped upper bodies and with vertical and horizontal painted stripes.

The one category of coarse-ware to undergo rapid change after the seventh century was lamp production. During the Middle Byzantine period, lamps of open form superseded the closed forms of the Early Byzantine period. These were often partly or wholly glazed and wheelmade. The most common form of lamp was an open dish, often with lobes, and a handle at its rear, but others with a dish on a 'stem' above a saucer-shaped base are also found. Olive oil was placed in the dish, with a floating wick, unlike the typical Early Byzantine lamp.

The fabric of Middle Byzantine coarse-wares is usually gritty and their surfaces frequently left plain, although smoothed. For example, very micaceous local coarse-ware, associated with Middle Byzantine glazed whiteware pottery, was found on the northern Greek island of Thassos. A red, orange or grey colour remained normal and the exterior of vessels was sometimes enhanced by burnished designs as it had been before the seventh century, as on the distinctive 'Red Burnished Ware' found at Istanbul. This was a gritty grey-brown fabric, poorly fired and used almost entirely for jugs (although other vessel forms are known), manufactured in or near the Byzantine capital.[13]

Constantinopolitan Greyware continued to be one of the principal coarse-wares used in Constantinople. The Early Byzantine version (Hayes Saraçhane wares 1 and 3) seems to develop through an eighth- to ninth-century fabric (Hayes Saraçhane ware 6), although these later forms have flat bottoms. Middle Byzantine Constantinopolitan Greyware is well made and clean of inclusions except for sand and a little limestone, although towards the end of the eleventh century it became coarser and thicker walled. Products include jars and, especially, cooking pots — their function evidenced by smoke-blackened sherds. Vessels sometimes carried external ribbing and incised decoration including lines and arcs, both continuing Early Byzantine coarse-ware decorative traditions.

Another important coarse-ware producer in Constantinople manufactured what is known as 'Constantinopolitan Whiteware' ('CWW'), a fabric also used for fine-ware production. Unglazed Constantinopolitan Whiteware ('UCWW') was primarily used for jugs and for lids to accompany these — although jars, bowls and other forms were also produced in the fabric. Unglazed Constantinopolitan Whiteware was manufactured from at least the seventh to twelfth centuries and, along with Saraçhane Greyware, was the main coarse-ware of the Middle Byzantine capital.

Unglazed Constantinopolitan Whiteware comprises five distinct fabrics, numbered here after the classification by Hayes in the Saraçhane excavation report. These fabrics parallel those of glazed Constantinopolitan Whiteware (also numbered following Hayes), discussed in the next chapter. UCWW1, dating from the seventh to the ninth century, is identical to CWW1. UCWW3 is identical to CWW2, and UCWW4 is equivalent to CWW3; these two fabrics date to the ninth to twelfth centuries. The last fabric, UCWW5, is equivalent to CWW4 and possibly related to CWW5. It probably belongs to the twelfth century.

The relationship of Constantinopolitan Whiteware to earlier pottery production in the City is unclear. It may well relate to a poorly understood group of Early Byzantine slipped whiteware, comprised of jugs, termed 'Colour Coated Whiteware' by Hayes. Colour Coated Whiteware is first evidenced *c*.500 at Saraçhane, although it might have originated in the fifth century. Like later Unglazed Constantinopolitan Whiteware, this has a soft white-pink fabric, colour-coated red, perhaps in imitation of Early Byzantine fine-wares. If achieving a red colour was the aim, it was sometimes a failure, because the true colour is often darker: orangey-brown or black.

Colour Coated Whiteware seems to disappear from the Constantinopolitan pottery-sequence just when Unglazed Constantinopolitan Whiteware is first recognizable. It seems possible, therefore, that it was the direct ancestor of UCWW and, if so, it should be categorized as the earliest variety of that class, although Hayes would separate these on the basis of the Saraçhane assemblages. However, if the ware does originate in the Early Byzantine period as suggested here, its origins and development would almost exactly parallel that of Constantinopolitan Greyware. However, Hayes would prefer to see the various greyware pottery grouped together under this class here as distinct products.

Together, interpreted in this way, they seem to provide evidence that coarse-wares deriving from local Late Roman ceramic traditions were manufactured in large quantities to serve the capital throughout the Middle Byzantine period. This long-lived production was, perhaps, only disrupted by the Latin occupation of Constantinople in 1204, after which there is no published evidence for continuing production of either Constantinopolitan Greyware or Unglazed Constantinopolitan Whiteware. That is, on this basis it might well be possible to argue that what was in origin 'Roman pottery' was produced and used in Constantinople until its capture by the Crusaders.

This is consistent with the overall suggestions of general continuity in coarse-ware production from the Early Byzantine period. Shapes, even precise forms, technology and decoration changed little from *c*.400-*c*.1200. This does not, of course, mean that no change at all had occurred. There had been changes in the details of form and decoration in most classes of coarse-ware, so that Middle Byzantine products are typologically recognisable. But how noticeable these gradual changes in the detail of vessels were to their Byzantine users it is far more difficult to say.

More importantly, new fabrics had been introduced, indicating new manufacturers or places of production, and long-established fabrics ceased production. A few distinctive products, such as Early Byzantine lamps, were no longer available. The picture is one of the continuity of a tradition of pottery-making rather than individual producers or the survival of archaic forms.

There is also evidence of artistic innovation by coarse-ware potters during the Middle Byzantine period, such as the beginning of a long-lived series of Matt-Painted coarse-wares produced in southern Greece. These were manufactured from the twelfth century onward and so are only found at the very end of the Middle Byzantine period. But they are extremely distinctive products, which seem a new departure in local ceramics. They are characterised by the use of red, white or brown painted decoration on an unglazed buff or even pink surface.[14]

Another change, also associated with southern Greece, is the appearance of handmade jars, in a dark grey fabric with combed external decoration and incised lines near the rim. This pottery is usually termed 'Slavic', but the name derives from the belief that such ceramics represent the pottery of an intrusive population group (the Slavs) within the Byzantine Empire. There is no unambiguous evidence that this is the case, and the class is termed here 'Handmade Ware'. Although many parts of the Roman Empire had handmade pottery traditions of their own, the so-called 'Slavic' wares represent an innovation in local ceramic production.[15]

It is possible that this pottery could be associated with the Slavic invasion, as the class was used for cremation urns at Olympia and was found associated with what might be Slavic occupation at Tiryns. This could support a connection with Slavic migrants as the origin of this pottery, but the class also occurs at Corinth, Isthmia and Argos where Slavic control seems unlikely. More problematical is evidence from the north Balkans that the Slavs produced no pottery of their own until the eighth century — long after the migration had ended and local Slavs were integrated into Byzantine society.

Chronological considerations also cast doubt upon the 'Slavic' attribution. Handmade Ware was associated with datable seventh-century pottery at Argos, and work at Nicopolis Ad Istrum in Bulgaria provides a *terminus post quem* of the late sixth century for similar material there. At Isthmia, Handmade Ware seems, at earliest, seventh-century and may have remained in use for a long period at the site. Handmade Ware seems, therefore, to belong to the late sixth century at earliest and probably began to be made in, or after, the seventh century. Similar pottery was produced in Bulgaria and the northern Balkans for centuries from the eighth century onwards and the material from within the Byzantine Empire might be of a similar date.

If it belongs to the eighth and later centuries, this material may relate to the Byzantine Empire's Bulgarian connections, rather the later sixth century Slavic migration. Most probably Handmade Ware represents, therefore, a class of Middle Byzantine pottery and is nothing to do with the sixth- or seventh-century Slavs. It potentially affords valuable information about the eighth- or ninth-century Balkan contacts of the Byzantine population of what is today Greece.

Despite these changes, Middle Byzantine coarse-wares as a whole seem to represent a continuation of Early Byzantine coarse-ware traditions. That is, they would appear to evidence the survival of everyday pottery-making on local (perhaps often village) level and, in many cases, local fabrics from the fifth to twelfth centuries. This pattern is also seen when we look at amphorae.

The Early Byzantine style of amphora, although not the specific classes, also continued in use into the seventh and eighth centuries. With the loss of Palestine, Egypt and North Africa in the seventh century, Byzantine amphora production unsurprisingly concentrated on the Aegean and Anatolia. Middle Byzantine amphorae remain super-ficially similar to Early Byzantine examples, but show more 'extremes' of design and decoration. For example, they have a more pro-nounced upward looping handle and often very low necks. Exteriors were still usually rilled or combed, and rilling sometimes extended over the whole exterior. Conversely, exam-ples without any external decoration are found.[16]

The most important work on Middle Byzantine amphorae has been by the Turkish scholar, Nergis

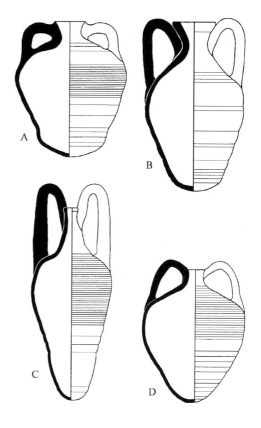

18 The main classes of Middle and Late Byzantine amphora. A Günsenin 1; B Günsenin 2; C Günsenin 3; D Günsenin 4. After Günsenin

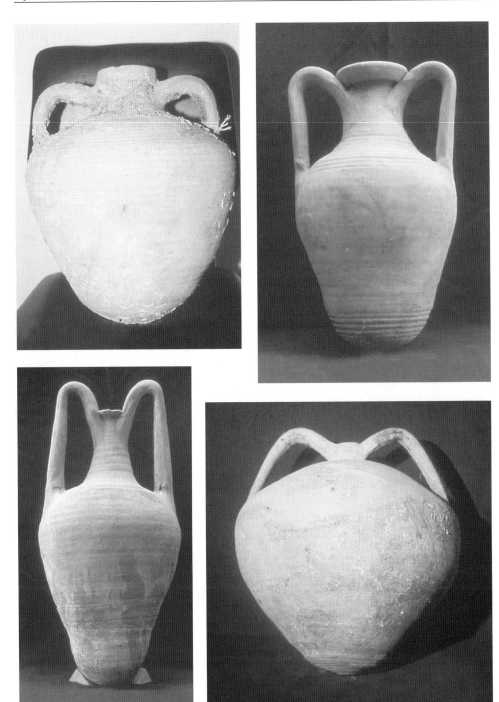

*19 Günsenin amphora types 1-4. Top left Günsenin 1; top right Günsenin 2;
bottom left Günsenin 3; bottom right Günsenin 4.*
Reproduced with kind permission of Dr Nergis Günsenin

Günsenin. She has grouped the most common Middle Byzantine amphorae into four classes, named after her. Günsenin 1 (dating from the ninth to eleventh centuries) comprises short-necked amphorae in a soft orange-red or light brown fabric with small D-shaped handles attached to rim and body, which is approximately pear-shaped. The upper part of the body is partially ribbed, while its lower portion is lower partially tegulated with a characteristic 'offset' carination.

Günsenin 2 (also dating from the ninth to eleventh centuries) are jar-like vessels in a light orange-brown fabric, with upward sloping handles attached to join of body and neck, and body where this is partially ribbed. The neck has a more flaring aperture than other Middle Byzantine types.

Günsenin 3 (perhaps dating from the eleventh to thirteenth centuries) has a soft pale brown fabric with darker surface and many organic voids. The exterior is frequently partially or entirely ribbed, and its lower portion may be partially tegulated. Günsenin 3 has pronounced upward-sloping handles attached to rim or top of the long neck and shoulder where it may be heavily ribbed.

Finally, Günsenin 4 (dating from the twelfth to thirteenth centuries) has a hard red, from maroon/orange-red fabric. It has slightly upward-sloping D-shaped handles attached to the rim above a short neck and the upper body, often where this is ribbed, although plain bodies are also known.

All of these classes seem to have been manufactured in Anatolia, but were probably more widely made in the Byzantine Empire. Hayes' work on amphorae from Saraçhane in Istanbul shows that a wider range of vessels were in use in the eighth to twelfth centuries, but Günsenin's work forms a useful basis for the future study of these.

The stamping of amphorae with symbols (often monograms or religious motifs), while also attested in the Early Byzantine period, is especially common in the Middle Byzantine period up to the eleventh century. These stamps have been found widely, but have never been thoroughly catalogued or analyzed and remain an untapped source of information about this period.

The size range of Middle Byzantine amphorae is also more 'extreme' than those of the early Byzantine period. Middle Byzantine amphorae were often either larger, or conversely much smaller, than Early Byzantine vessels. Once more, the moderation of Early Byzantine amphora production was discarded, to produce less technically accomplished but more 'exaggerated' vessels. This reduction of technical quality is accompanied by a far more limited distribution, concentrating on the lands under Middle Byzantine control and eastern Europe.

This suggests that, as with the other coarse-wares, overall continuity coexisted with innovation. Innovation in the range of non-ceramic containers used for transport also affected the use of amphorae. From the tenth century onward, amphorae were in greater competition with wooden barrels as means of transporting bulk goods, perhaps as a result of Western trading connections. This Western connection is also seen in relation to Byzantine amphorae in the ninth century, when the change in the usual shape of the body of Italian amphorae from oval to spherical is perhaps mirrored in Byzantine amphora manufacture.

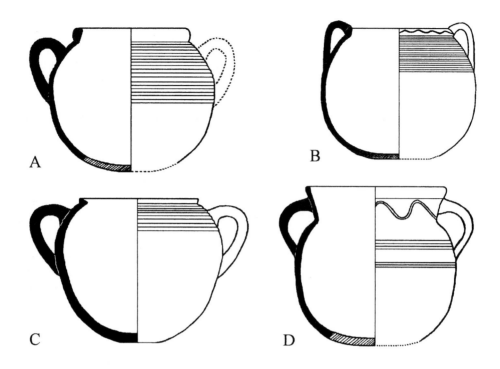

20 Examples of forms of Late Byzantine coarse-wares from Corinth.
    After Stillwell-Mackay

To summarise, we can see both continuity and innovation as Early Byzantine pottery shapes and manufacturing techniques remained in use, but new fabrics, forms and decorative styles were introduced. The most credible interpretation may be that Middle Byzantine coarse-wares represent the direct continuation of the Early Byzantine coarse-ware tradition within the reduced extent of the Byzantine Empire, alongside ongoing innovation and experimentation by the local potters producing them.

Late Byzantine coarse-wares

A profound change in coarse-ware manufacture seems to have occurred after the thirteenth century. In Constantinople, Middle Byzantine coarse-wares were replaced after the mid-thirteenth century by grey and red fabrics unlike those of the period before *c.*1200. Although vessel shapes remain similar, technically this is much poorer quality pottery and it seems from these differences that coarse-ware production in the capital may have been disrupted. This disruption may also be detected in thirteenth-century Corinth.[17]

Few thirteenth- and fourteenth-century cooking pots are known from most of Greece and the remaining Byzantine territories in Anatolia. The Anatolian products of these centuries seem to include globular pots with vertical strap-handles attached to the rim and the rilled body, in hard-fired gritty and highly micaceous red-brown fabrics. These were imported into Byzantine controlled areas of Greece, such as Corinth.

In Greece, almost all the known well-dated examples (as at Agios Stephanos in southern Greece) are either glazed or unglazed 'frying pans' or globular unglazed vessels with flat bottoms or low bases and horizontal loop handles and often with everted rims. At Corinth, more vertically-rimmed cooking pits are found and at Athens two-handled long-necked jars with horizontal applied bands of pinched decoration perhaps belong to this period. At Sparta, fourteenth-century cooking pots in grey or brown fabrics with round bottoms appear to be more similar to Middle Byzantine vessels.

Matt-Painted Ware became especially common across southern Greece (as at Corinth and Mistra), from the late thirteenth century onwards. To give an example, Guy Sanders has calculated that 87 per cent of the Late Byzantine coarse-wares at Corinth was Matt-Painted Ware. Matt-Painted Ware open vessels in hard, gritty pink-brown, reddish-yellow or buff fabric occur for the first time in the thirteenth century. The style of decoration of matt-painted pottery changes, with the simple linear designs of the twelfth century abandoned for herring-bone patterns and red paint more frequently used than white. A local product of this period is the series of so-called 'Lakonian Amphorae', defined by Pamela Armstrong. These are amphora-like jars (*stamnia*), produced in a buff fabric and with very distinctive diagonally-slashed handles. They are found, exclusively it seems, it southern and central Greece and a complete vessel of this class, with multiple handles, is recorded from Sparta.[18]

Incised and relief-decorated unglazed cooking pots and jugs were manufactured in a Late, or possibly post-, Byzantine context on Keos, and globular handled cooking pots and jugs with incised decoration were produced in red-brown fabrics in Crete. But, on the whole, after the mid-thirteenth century the character of Byzantine coarse-ware production in the eastern Mediterranean islands is unclear.

Late Byzantine coarse-wares might also be argued to exhibit more similarities to western European pottery than did Middle Byzantine vessels. For example, cooking pots show higher necks and new rim-forms after *c.*1250 in Corinth, a change that was so sudden that it has been attributed to the influx of Westerners to the city after the fall of Constantinople to the Byzantines in 1261. Even the popularity of Matt-Painted Ware may be related to the fashion for this in southern Italy in the thirteenth century, but whether this was copying Byzantine tastes or the opposite remains uncertain. Late Byzantine jugs too — including very dark green glazed vessels in red-brown fabrics — now sometimes had the lobed mouths and longer necks of Italian medieval vessels.

Late Byzantine amphorae occur in smaller sizes, smaller quantities and fewer classes than Middle Byzantine products. Barrels were in common use for purposes formerly fulfilled by amphorae, although the latter were still used for special products — probably including the famous wine ('Malmsey') of Monemvasia in southern Greece. Small amphorae of thirteenth- and fourteenth-century date found at Mistra and elsewhere in the Peloponesse may, as Guy Sanders suggests, have served this function.[19]

While upward-sloping handles continue to be the most distinctive feature of the amphorae, the shape of these is usually more spherical — or conversely more tubular — than Middle Byzantine examples. They have a far more emphatic 'shoulder', with handles joining at the neck. Rilling is rarer than before, although it still covers the outside of some examples. These amphorae remain widespread, attesting to the vitality of trade.

Amphora seems to have passed from use during the fourteenth century, finally being superceded by wooden containers (*voutsia*). This change marks the end of a long tradition of amphora use and a profound change in the material culture of the Byzantine world.

In summary, a discontinuity in coarse-ware production may have occurred in the thirteenth century. Ceramics were less extensively used and new vessel shapes introduced.

Conclusion

Early Byzantine coarse-wares represent a continuation of Roman traditions, usually without major changes in shape, decoration or fabric. Middle Byzantine coarse-wares continue this pattern of overall continuity into the twelfth century, albeit with more evidence of changes in the detail of vessel form and decoration. The use of new fabrics and other innovations that attest a living — and not deliberately conservative — coarse-ware ceramic tradition. This could represent the partial survival of Late Roman patterns of pottery-use to *c*.1200, when a striking discontinuity occurs during the thirteenth century. This is followed by the reduction of ceramic use and the cessation of these long-standing traditions. When Constantinople fell in 1453, coarse-ware pottery was probably less widely used by its Byzantine inhabitants than before the thirteenth century. By that time, pottery-manufacturing no longer preserved traditions traceable back to the Early Byzantine period. Presumably, this suggests that the ways of life associated with these, too, may not have survived beyond *c*.1200 or perhaps, more precisely, for long after the Latin Empire was established.

3 Byzantine fine-wares: pottery as periodization

Introduction

A different pattern of development is seen in relation to Byzantine fine-wares. Most Byzantine settlements probably had some fine-ware pottery and, although only a few fine-ware sherds may be found on rural sites, these are often much more closely datable than coarse-wares. Consequently, at many sites, fine-wares provide a way of dating both archaeological layers in excavation and scatters of pottery found on the modern ground surface.

Intriguingly, each of the main periods of Byzantine political history has its own 'signature' group of fine-wares, so that fine-ware production seems to run parallel to broader trends in Byzantine political and cultural history. It is, therefore, worth discussing this sequence of Byzantine fine-wares in chronological order to investigate the relationship between each stage of development.

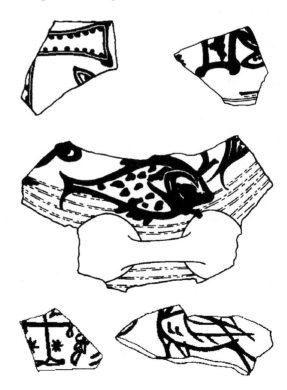

21 Monastic Ware. Reproduced with the kind permission of Mark Jackson

22 Early Byzantine Egyptian Painted Ware. Reproduced with the kind permission of The British Museum

Early Byzantine fine-wares

The main fifth- to seventh-century fine-wares comprise unglazed painted vessels and, especially, unglazed red-slipped wares. A small quantity of other fine-wares, notably an enigmatic mica-dusted red ware, were also produced, but these seem to have been supplementary 'exotic' products or for specific purposes.[1]

Early Byzantine painted wares were not usually traded over long distances. Thus, while numerous in their 'home' areas, they are seldom encountered elsewhere. Such wares include 'Coptic' Egyptian Painted Ware, Monastic Ware in Anatolia and the 'Jerash Bowls' (thin-walled red-slipped painted wares with figural or floral decoration in purple or yellow-cream) found in what is today Jordan. These classes remain poorly understood compared to the red-slipped wares that tend to dominate publications of Early Byzantine pottery.[2]

From the fifth to seventh century, a standardized range of unglazed red-slipped fine-wares was produced by a small number of large-scale industries. These were very widely traded and swamped the Mediterranean fine-ware pottery market. Such products (and local imitations of them) are virtually universal on sites of this date throughout the Byzantine Empire, whatever their function or status, and whether secular or religious in character. They provided a high quality, durable and (at least to a modern observer) attractive set of smooth (sometimes glossy) surfaced red-coloured table pottery, suitable for dining and display. Red-slipped fine-wares were undoubtedly the most common good quality tableware in the Early Byzantine Empire.

The derivation and origins of the main Early Byzantine fine-wares are not in doubt. They lie in the Late Roman fine-ware traditions of the Eastern Roman Empire itself. That is, these Early Byzantine fine-wares represent the continuing production of pre-*c*.400 ceramics.

Although red-slipped wares constituted a shared Early Byzantine tradition of pottery use, particular wares within their range were all associated with particular regions. Each major supplier, probably a cluster of producers rather than a single 'firm', served an extensive market in their own and neighbouring areas. It is also important to note that Early Byzantine red-slipped wares represent the last stage of a long-lasting taste for such pottery in the Roman world as a whole, most notably including the well-known *terra sigillata* (samian ware) popular in the Early Roman West. It appears that the 'Roman' character of Early Byzantine red-slipped fine-wares, like that of Early Byzantine coarse-wares, is assured.

Despite this regionalization, the degree of standardization of Early Byzantine red-slip wares

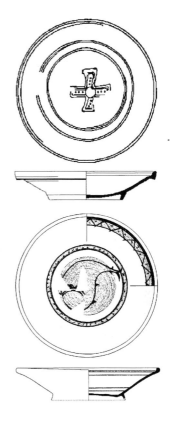

23 'Jerash Bowls'.
After Watson

is one of its most striking features. Not only was it all approximately 'red' in colour, but a limited range of shapes and decorative styles existed. Within this general consistency of appearance, red-slipped wares were affected by rapid changes from one precise vessel-form to another, permitting very accurate dating.

The most common Early Byzantine fine-ware shapes were broad shallow plates and bowls. Closed forms, such as jugs, were also produced. Lamps derivative of earlier Roman shapes were also made in fine-ware fabrics during the Early Byzantine period, but have been discussed in the previous chapter.

Painted fine-wares played only a subsidiary role to the products of the few large-scale 'industries' manufacturing this red-slipped pottery. Local imitations of red-slipped fine-ware (showing that supply could not fulfil demand) were manufactured rather than use the local painted equivalents. For example, at Anemurium, Cypriot Red Slip Ware and Phocaean Red Slip Ware were both copied in local pinkish-brown or orange fabrics. However, none of these copies was manufactured in sufficient quantity to displace the central role of the pottery it emulated.[3]

The fine-ware of the Early Byzantine Empire was, therefore, largely comprised of red-slipped vessels of 'Roman' appearance, produced in a few centres and

24 *African Red Slip Ware plate.* Reproduced with the kind permission of The British Museum

traded and imitated across the Empire. This was supplemented by local painted fine-wares, but none of these painted wares became common outside the area in which it was produced.

This provided the entire Early Byzantine Empire with a supply of good quality table-ware, and the commonness of this pottery attests that this was available to most of the Early Byzantine population. The cessation of the extensive use of these fine-wares broadly coincided with the collapse of Byzantine rule in Palestine, Egypt and North Africa in the seventh century. Although production of Byzantine-style fine-wares continued locally (notably in Egypt) for a century or more after Byzantine rule ceased, these were no longer widely traded even inside the Empire after the seventh century.

However, the end of Byzantine rule in Palestine and North Africa does not explain why red-slipped wares lost their commercial dominance in the seventh century, even if these two changes coincided. Although some of the most widely used fine-wares were made in North Africa, others were produced in areas that remained under Byzantine rule. For example, Phoceaen Red Slip Ware and Sagalassos Red Slip Ware were produced in western Anatolia, which remained firmly within the Empire during the seventh and eighth centuries. Yet neither was manufactured after the seventh century.

It is often claimed that difficulties in sea travel explain the collapse of long distance pottery trade in the seventh century. Although the long sea journey from Carthage to Constantinople may have become more hazardous, relatively short land and sea routes remained possible that would have enabled Phoceaen Red Slip Ware manufacturers to reach much of what was left of the Byzantine Empire. As such alternative supplies were not exploited, it seems unlikely that communication problems led to the cessation of red-slip ware use.

It may be more likely that the disuse of red-slipped fine-ware in the Byzantine Empire has an explanation in cultural change, rather than in economic or military terms. The explanation of this change will be discussed in greater length later in this book, but here it is worth noting that it is possible that an association between red-slipped pottery and Roman identity may have promoted both the use of these fine-wares and led to their eventual demise.

An explanation based on cultural change may also enable us to understand why painted unglazed fine-wares too were no longer used within the Byzantine Empire after the seventh century. Local fine-wares of this sort, common throughout the fifth and sixth centuries in Anatolia for example, seem to disappear from archaeological visibility during the seventh century. Outside the Empire, some formerly

25 Glazed Constantinopolitan Whiteware from the Great Palace of Byzantine Constantinople in The British Museum. The glaze is pale yellow

26 One of the earliest known glazed vessels in the Byzantine Empire. Glazed bowl from Yassı Ada II. Courtesy of the Institute of Nautical Archaeology

Byzantine populations retained a painted fine-ware tradition, as among the Christian 'Coptic' population of Egypt. Perhaps these communities maintained — or even enhanced — the identities expressed by this pottery during the seventh and later centuries, relatively unaffected by changes in imperial borders.

The declining popularity of red-slipped wares led to the proliferation of new fine-wares. These were the glazed vessels that represent the fine-ware 'signature' of the Middle Byzantine period.

Middle Byzantine fine-wares

In *c*.600, the only widespread fine-wares were unglazed red-slip ware vessels with red fabrics but by *c*.800 the only widespread fine-wares were glazed wares, often with a white or pink fabric. This both offers an easy way of differentiating Early Byzantine and Middle Byzantine fine-ware and poses a puzzle as to how this transformation occurred.

The origins of Byzantine glazed pottery

It is uncertain when and where the first Byzantine glazed pottery was produced. It is often said that the first well-dated Byzantine glazed pottery is that in the Yassı Ada II wreck (*c*.625-6) and glazed whiteware is found after *c*.600 in Constantinople itself, as at Saraçhane. Similar material from elsewhere in the eastern Mediterranean is dated to the seventh and eighth centuries.[4]

It is not absolutely certain that any of this represents the earliest Byzantine glazed pottery. For example, what appears to be glazed pottery dating has been found at St Lot's Monastery at Deir ain' Abata in Jordan. This well-excavated Early Byzantine church has what might be green-glazed vessels that seem to be

27 Seventh-century glazed redware from the Great Palace at Constantinople, in The British Museum

contemporary with Early Byzantine red-slipped finewares. Elsewhere in Byzantine Palestine seventh- and eighth-century two-handled cooking pots were sometimes lead-glazed, and Caroline Williams has drawn attention to lead-glazed shallow cooking vessels from Early Byzantine deposits at Caesarea Maritima. So it is possible that glazed pottery was already used, albeit in small quantities, in Early Byzantine Palestine.[5]

Turquoise glazed pottery was produced in Syria from the Late Roman period through to the early Islamic period. These turquoise glazed wares were produced alongside other Byzantine fine-wares in western Anatolia later in the Byzantine period, as evidence at Sardis has demonstrated, but any link between these two phases of production remains unclear. Whatever the relationship between this and later glazed pottery, the existence of these Early Byzantine vessels extends further northward the possible zone in which Early Byzantine glazed wares were manufactured.[6]

It seems that glazed pottery was also used in Early Byzantine Anatolia. Another potentially sixth-century glazed vessel was found in the excavation of Byzantine shops at Sardis, although this too could belong to the seventh century and glazed pottery was also in use at Anemurium by the seventh century, if not already in the sixth. Again, these products are only present at each site in very small quantities, but they may suggest that glazed pottery manufacture was more widespread in the Early Byzantine Empire than is usually supposed.[7]

It is unclear whether a similar glazed pottery-making tradition existed in Early Byzantine Greece. Glazed jugs were manufactured in Athens in the fourth and fifth centuries and the small-scale use of glazing may be attested on fifth-century lamps from Athens. Further north in the Balkans, in what is today Bulgaria, glazed ceramics may have been produced in the fourth to fifth century, as George Kuzmanov argued. So, the sixth- and seventh-century survival of a minor local tradition of glazed pottery-production remains a possibility in these areas too.[8]

This provides a previously unappreciated context for the seventh-century emergence of the 'classic' Middle Byzantine glazed wares in Constantinople. It is possible that there was an, as yet largely unrecognized, continuous fifth- and sixth-century glazed pottery tradition in the Byzantine Empire. To judge from excavated sites, glazed vessels of this early date were rare enough to have been overlooked at other sites, or assigned later dates simply on the grounds of their glaze.

The existence of glazed pottery production at this date would not be unique. Locally-produced green-glazed pottery was also in use in Italy from *c*.400 at Ravenna and the neighbouring port at Classe. Glazed pottery was also made elsewhere in northern Italy and lead-glazed yellow and green coloured vessels were produced in southern and central Italy by the seventh century at the latest.[9]

Thus although red-slipped wares were the most widely used sixth- and seventh-century fine-wares in Italy, glazed pottery is well-attested there before *c*.600, and was widespread by the seventh century. As John Hayes has pointed out, these Italian glazed wares are a possible source for the earliest Byzantine glazed wares of Constantinople, if one imagines the transfer of that technology from Ravenna to the Byzantine capital in the seventh century.

It is therefore possible that the origin of Byzantine glazed pottery might be sought within the Byzantine Empire itself, perhaps being transferred to the capital by seventh-century refugees from the provinces. Alternatively, potters or technologies might have arrived in Constantinople from Italy after Byzantine rule was established in this area. Both explanations would fit the chronology of Byzantine glazed pottery in Constantinople very well. An Italian connection might also explain the production of Petal Ware in Middle Byzantine Constantinople, when its closest analogy is the 'Forum Ware' pottery of Italy. However, it is unclear whether any Forum Ware pre-dates the earliest Byzantine Petal Ware.[10]

Another option that has not yet been discussed is that Byzantine and Italian potters might themselves have invented the use of glaze at broadly the same time in several different locations. This could have occurred because of the regular juxtaposition of glass-working and pottery manufacture, creating a context in which technologies could simply be transferred from one 'industry' to the other. If such juxtaposition was commonplace, then this innovation could have occurred in several places over a short period of time. So, the near-simultaneous introduction of the glazing process is possible without evoking extremes of chance.

It is difficult to explore this latter hypothesis further due to a lack of evidence about sixth- and seventh-century pottery-making establishments and their environs. At present, we are forced to use only the pottery itself as evidence in any attempt to choose between these options. Most discussion of the earliest Middle Byzantine glazed pottery has naturally focused on the use of glaze, but another approach is to look at its other distinctive characteristics.

Apart from glazing, all the technological characteristics of the earliest Middle Byzantine glazed fine-wares are found also in Early Byzantine products. Incised decoration, stamping and rouletting occur on Early Byzantine painted wares from Anatolia. Further details found on Middle Byzantine glazed pottery can also be paralleled on Early Byzantine coarse-wares from the same area, such as finger-impressed ornament on the local ware found at Anemurium in southern Anatolia.[11]

Thus, while the characteristic glazed whiteware products of the Middle Byzantine capital appear at first sight very dissimilar to Early Byzantine fine-wares, a closer examination shows that this is not always the case. The red-slipped Early Byzantine fine-ware in a whiteware fabric found at Saraçhane demonstrates that a red-slipped fine-ware with a whiteware body was used, and perhaps produced, in Constantinople.[12]

Middle Byzantine glazed whitewares often carry a well-finished red slip under the glaze and on the surfaces left unglazed. If one mentally 'removes' the glaze, they would closely resemble these red-slipped wares. That is, the only technological change that has to have occurred in the seventh century in order to create the characteristic Middle Byzantine white-fabric fine-ware of the capital, was the addition of a lead glaze to existing fine-ware products.

The existence of these characteristics found in Middle Byzantine glazed pottery within the repertoire of Early Byzantine potters strengthens the case that this originated in the local pottery-producing traditions of the eastern Mediterranean. But this does not explain why glazing is first evidenced in relatively minor local products. It is possible that the answer to this question indeed lies in the juxtaposition of glass- and pottery-manufacture.

As will be discussed later, large-scale red-slipware producers probably had more specialised pottery-making establishments than did local manufacturers operating from small workshops. If so, then the major fine-ware 'industries' perhaps provided less opportunity for the juxtaposition of potting and other activities such as glass-making. Consequently, one would expect that the transfer of glazing technology would occur at the smaller-scale workshops.

The small-scale local production of glazed coarse-wares in the Early Byzantine period, resulting from technology-transfer between glass-manufacture and potting at minor local potteries, may therefore explain the origins of Middle Byzantine glazed ceramics. However, it is difficult to exclude some relationship between the origins of Byzantine glazed pottery and the origins of glazed pottery in Italy. But whatever the exact nature of these Italian connections, it seems most likely that the origins of Byzantine glazed pottery lie within the Empire itself.

This raises the possibility that the sixth-century Byzantine conquest of Italy enabled the pre-existing Italian tradition of glazed ceramics (perhaps originating in a similar juxtaposition of potting and glass-making) to be combined with Byzantine innovations. If so, then there might well be a much greater Byzantine contribution to the development of medieval Italian — and by extension other western European — glazed pottery than has hitherto been supposed. In this context, Forum Ware might provide a crucial link between the two areas and may well repay further investigation from this perspective.

Although found in Italy, the development of glazed pottery was not immediately shared by neighbouring peoples in the eastern Mediterranean. There was no Islamic glazed pottery before *c*.700; the nearest area to the east of the Byzantine Empire in which glazed pottery was commonly used prior to *c*.700 was China. Islamic glazed pottery is first found during the Abbassid period in Mesopotamia and is extremely rare elsewhere in the Middle East before the eighth century.[13]

Eighth- to tenth-century Abbassid glazed ceramics have some similarities to contemporary Byzantine products. They include stamped and relief-moulded lead glazed jars, bowls and plates with moulded and incised decoration, under transparent, green or coloured glazes. Arabic script is frequently incorporated into the designs and ninth- and tenth-century Abassid products have prominent animal and even human designs in the centre of the interior. This contrasts with decoration on the earliest Byzantine glazed pottery and Abassid vessels were usually glazed only on the interior, whereas Byzantine glazed ceramics were glazed on the exterior also.

Another difference between Middle Byzantine glazed fine-wares and Islamic glazed pottery is the absence of true 'Lustre' glazing. Lustre wares used a tin-glaze to give a thin metallic film with a distinctive glossy appearance. Blue painted tin-glazed pottery was used in ninth-century Mesopotamia but 'true' Lustre Ware is first found in that area in the tenth century. The Byzantines were aware of Lustre Ware, as both imports found within the Empire and Imitation Lustre Ware show, but it seems that they never manufactured it. The absence of tin-glaze from Byzantine ceramics, although so commonplace in Islamic glazed pottery, further emphasises the separation of the two ceramic traditions.[14]

Moreover, the two ceramic traditions remained largely distinctive throughout the ninth to twelfth centuries. The rise of the Samanid dynasty united Persia east of the Oxus after 874 and was accompanied by a shift in pottery production to Nishapur and Samarkand. Samanid-period pottery is characterized by the manufacture of imitations of Chinese products, mostly in tin-glazed whitewares with cobalt blue or red, brown, white or black painted designs. These look very different both from Abbassid ceramics and from Middle Byzantine pottery.

It was a Byzantine innovation, therefore, that produced the first glazed pottery outside East Asia to gain as wide a circulation as the finest unglazed wares of its time. Within a century the fine-ware of the Arab world too was dominated by glazed pottery, but this was a later development. The origins of Abbassid glazed pottery could represent a completely independent phase of innovation, or the copying of Chinese ceramics. The well-attested tendency of the seventh- and eighth-century Arab elite to look to Byzantine artistic models raises the possibility that it might have resulted (at least in part) from the emulation of seventh- or eighth-century Byzantine glazed fine-wares.

There is also evidence that formerly Byzantine communities were among the first in the Arab-controlled Mediterranean to produce glazed pottery. In Egypt, the manufacture of 'Coptic' glazed wares began in the eighth century and glazed fine-ware is found at eighth-century Fustat (Old Cairo).[15]

The adoption of glazed wares also opened Byzantine potters to new possibilities of incorporating technical and artistic influences from China. From the T'ang period of Chinese history onwards, Chinese ceramics seem to have recognizable influence on both Byzantine and Islamic pottery, affecting decoration and shape alike. Middle Byzantine glazed pottery did not, therefore, develop in isolation but Byzantine potters learnt techniques and motifs from other manufacturers beyond imperial borders: Italy, China and eventually the Islamic world.[16]

Thus, it is possible to suggest a new explanation for the origins of Byzantine glazed pottery, placing its origins within the Empire. Moreover, the Byzantines were the first people in the Middle East to adopt glazed pottery for the majority of fine-wares and this may have played a key role in initiating the later Middle Eastern (and perhaps western European) glazed pottery traditions. This development shows that at least some Byzantine potters were technologically innovative, despite the conservatism found in relation to coarse-ware production.

The classic Middle Byzantine fine-wares

The glazed pottery that became the standard fine-ware of the Middle Byzantine Empire was the glazed whiteware already mentioned. This comprised a series of related fabrics, which probably began to be used for glazed fine-wares in the seventh century. They have a characteristic white or pink colour and are decorated with painted, incised or stamped (usually called 'impressed') designs. In Constantinople itself, glazed whitewares of this sort remained the main fine-wares of the eighth to twelfth centuries and one fabric 'Constantinopolitan whiteware' (CWW) was produced in or near the city from the seventh century until at least *c.*1200.[17]

Genuine Constantinopolitan products seem to occur at Thessaloniki and at Thassos, Samothrace, Melos and Xanthos, at Iznik in Anatolia and in Thrace. This suggests a northern route for their distribution from Constantinople along the coast to Greece. At least one of the several Middle Byzantine whiteware fabrics at Corinth and Cyprus may also be genuinely Constantinopolitan. Their outlying positions in the distribution pattern might suggest another route across the Aegean, perhaps direct from the capital.

Much confusion has arisen in previous studies of this pottery because of the assumption that all Middle Byzantine glazed whitewares are identical. This has led to virtually every whiteware sherd being equated with the whitewares found in Istanbul. But both laboratory-based examination and 'macroscopic' inspection demonstrate that whitewares were produced in several places. One of these places was in Constantinople (where wasters have been found) but there were also other centres of glazed whiteware production, notably in southern Greece and at Iznik in western Anatolia. For example, at Corinth a local whiteware copying CWW was probably manufactured from the eleventh century onward. At this time too, copies of CWW forms were also produced in other local fabrics, with form alone imitating CWW.[18]

By far the most elaborate, and presumably most expensive, of these glazed whitewares was Polychrome Ware, used for plates, bowls, cups and tiles. This is distinguished by (usually geometric or floral) designs in multicoloured paint on the white surface. A few examples have Greek inscriptions painted onto them and fewer still have gold powder or leaf applied to the surface prior to glazing, although this seems to be a specifically Constantinopolitan characteristic, possibly even associated with the Imperial Court.[19]

Polychrome Ware may be described in Theophilus's *De Diversis Artibus* II.16. This says that the Byzantines

> . . . make pottery dishes . . . and paint them like this. They take all sorts of colours and crush them separately with water. With each colour they mix a fifth part of glass of the same shade, which is also reduced to powder in water. With that they paint circles, arcs, rectangles and within these, animals, birds, foliage or some other subject. When the pots are painted like this, they put them in a glassmaker's furnace . . .

Only Polychrome Ware would fit this description.[20]

Polychrome Ware is widely, but 'thinly', distributed across the Empire, with small quantities found in most areas under Byzantine control when it was produced. It was also copied in Bulgaria, and might bear some relationship to the origins of Proto-Maiolica pottery in Italy. The latter is a white-bodied, polychrome painted, glazed fine-ware, which began production (probably in Apulia) at the start of the thirteenth century — exactly when Polychrome Ware production comes to an end in the Byzantine Empire. Proto-Maiolica vessels became widely used in the Late Byzantine world, perhaps replacing Polychrome Ware.[21]

A possible relationship between Polychrome Ware and Proto-Maiolica pottery (which played a central role in ceramic development in Renaissance Italy) appears to have previously escaped notice. However, Proto-Maiolica vessels share several similarities with Polychrome Ware. Both are predominantly 'white' coloured, have mostly (but not exclusively) geometric designs, sometimes carry pseudo-Kufic decoration, and are painted with a similar palette of colours. In more detail, they share several distinctive motifs, such as a 'peacock' design of eye-shaped manganese dots, a 'gridiron' hatched motif, and two unusual cross motifs. The first has each end of an equal-armed cross, bisected by a line forming a smaller cross, the second employs an equal-armed cross with dots between each of the arms.

Chronology makes it impossible that Polychrome Ware was a copy of Proto-Maiolica pottery, but the involvement of Italians in the Middle Byzantine economy would have provided plenty of opportunities to see and obtain Polychrome Ware. Intriguingly, in this context, the earliest dated Proto-Maiolica pottery is still that at Corinth, despite more than half a century of study, although it is plainly an Italian product.

The main obstacle to seeing a link between Proto-Maiolica pottery and Polychrome Ware is that the former is characteristically tin-glazed, probably emulating Islamic Lustre wares. However, lead-glazed products in a related tradition are known, for example from Tuscany, and the use of tin-glazing could have been intended to achieve a white finish emulating the whiter clays of Polychrome Ware. Thus, although the origins of Proto-Maiolica pottery drew on

1 *African Red Slip Ware plate in The British Museum*

2 *Early Byzantine red-slip ware plate and coarseware cup from the galley of the shipwreck at Yassı Ada II.* Courtesy of the Institute of Nautical Archaeology

3   Early Byzantine Egyptian Painted Ware. Reproduced with the kind permission of The British Museum

4   Early Byzantine Egyptian Painted Ware base sherd in the Victoria and Albert Museum

5   *Early Byzantine cooking pot in The British Museum*

6   *Early Byzantine amphora in The British Museum*

7 *Early Byzantine Rouletted Bowl and Rilled Rim Basin sherds from Jerusalem.*
Reproduced with the kind permission of Jodi Magness

8 *Early Byzantine pottery from Jerusalem, showing red-slipped fine-ware, coarse-wares
and lamp.* Reproduced with the kind permission of Jodi Magness

9   *Early Byzantine amphorae lying on the sea-bed at the shipwreck site at Yassı Ada II.*
Courtesy of the Institute of Nautical Archaeology

10 Reconstruction of the galley area of the Early Byzantine shipwreck at Yassı Ada II.
  Courtesy of the Institute of Nautical Archaeology

11 Middle Byzantine Plain Redware cup from Corinth. The American School of
Classical Studies, Corinth Excavations, taken from *Corinth XI*, by C. Morgan

12 Middle Byzantine Plain Redware cup from Corinth, showing relief decoration. The
American School of Classical Studies, Corinth Excavations, taken from
Corinth XI, by C.Morgan

13 Middle Byzantine cooking pots.
   Courtesy of the Institute of Nautical Archaeology

14 Late Byzantine Matt Painted coarseware vessels from Sparta in the Victoria and Albert
   Museum

15 *Middle Byzantine Constantinopolitan Glazed Whiteware from the Great Palace of Byzantine Constantinople, showing range of glaze colours used, in The British Museum*

16 *(above left) Middle Byzantine Petal Ware, a typical sherd, probably from Istanbul*
17 *(above right) Middle Byzantine Constantinopolitan Glazed Whiteware sherd, probably from Istanbul, showing incised decoration*

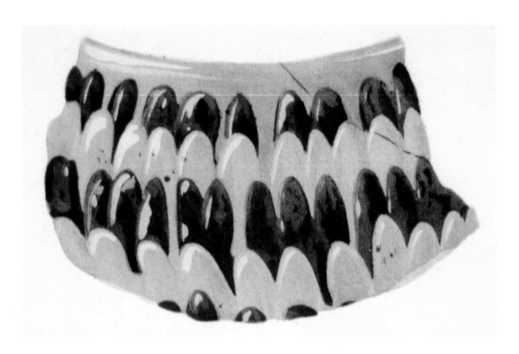

18 Middle Byzantine Petal Ware bowl from Corinth. The American School of Classical Studies, Corinth Excavations, taken from *Corinth XI*, by C. Morgan

19 Middle Byzantine glazed whiteware plate from Corinth. The American School of Classical Studies, Corinth Excavations, taken from *Corinth XI*, by C. Morgan

20 Middle Byzantine glazed Whiteware cup from Corinth. The American School of
Classical Studies, Corinth Excavations, taken from *Corinth XI*, by C. Morgan

21 Middle Byzantine glazed Whiteware 'fruit stand' from Corinth. The American School
of Classical Studies, Corinth Excavations, taken from *Corinth XI*, by C. Morgan

22 Middle Byzantine Constantinoplitan Whiteware base sherd with Greek inscription (phos zoe — 'light of life') and 'victory wreath', probably from Istanbul

23 Middle Byzantine Impressed Ware whiteware sherd possibly depicting a domed church, probably from Istanbul

24 Middle Byzantine 'Impressed Ware' whiteware bowls from Corinth. The American
School of Classical Studies, Corinth Excavations, taken from *Corinth XI*, by
C. Morgan

25 Middle Byzantine Polychrome Ware (group 1) vessels from Corinth. The American School of Classical Studies, Corinth Excavations, taken from *Corinth XI*, by C. Morgan

26 Middle Byzantine Polychrome Ware (group 1) plate rim-sherd with fragmentary Greek inscription, probably from Istanbul

27 *Middle Byzantine Polychrome Ware (groups 2 and 3) vessels (sherds) from Corinth.* The American School of Classical Studies, Corinth Excavations, taken from *Corinth XI*, by C. Morgan

28 *Typical cross designs found on Middle Byzantine Polychrome Ware. The sherd on the right was probably manufactured at Sparta. In the Victoria and Albert Museum*

29 *Bulgarian imitation of Middle Byzantine Polychrome Ware tile, in the Victoria and Albert Museum*

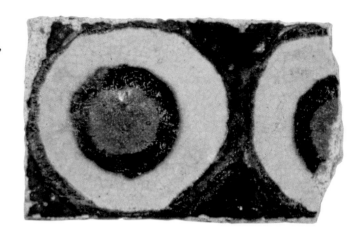

30 Polychrome Ware tile, from Istanbul

31 Polychrome Ware tile with gold leaf decoration from Istanbul

32 Polychrome Ware tile waster sherd, probably from Istanbul

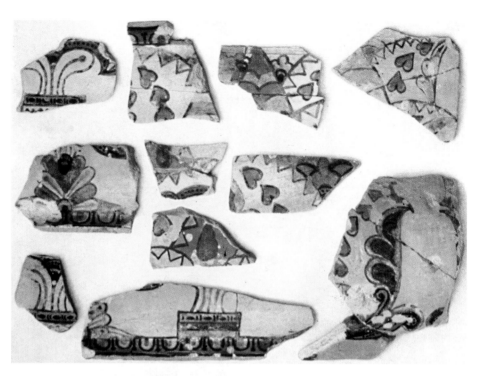

33-4 Bulgarian imitations of Middle Byzantine Polychrome Ware tiles. By David Talbot Rice, reproduced with the kind permission of the Talbot Rice family

35 *Polychrome ceramic icon from Veliki Preslav in Bulgaria. Similar icons were produced inside the Byzantine Empire.* Painting by David Talbot Rice, reproduced with the kind permission of the Talbot Rice family

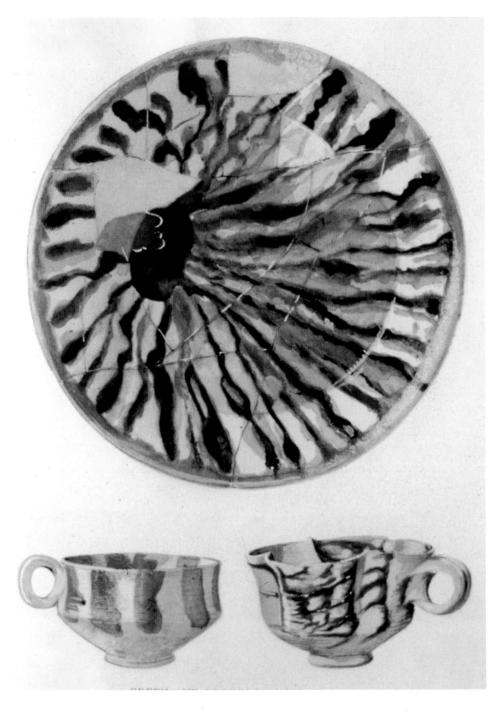

36 Middle Byzantine Green and Brown Painted Ware vessels from Corinth. The American School of Classical Studies, Corinth Excavations, taken from *Corinth XI*, by C. Morgan

37 Middle Byzantine Imitation Lustre Ware plate from Corinth. The American School of Classical Studies, Corinth Excavations, taken from *Corinth XI*, by C. Morgan

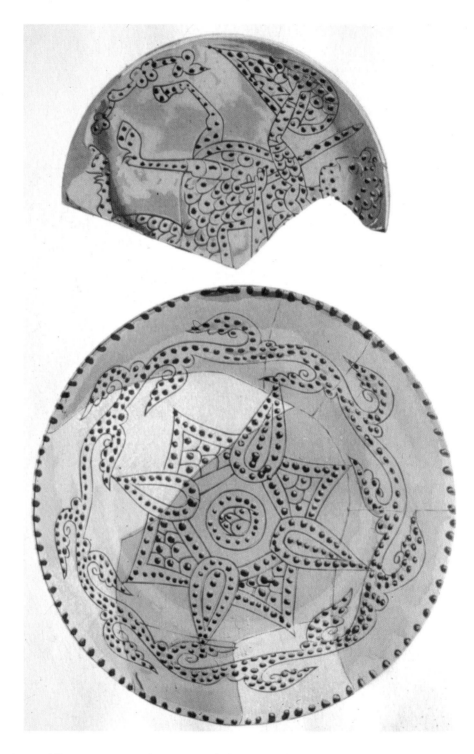

38 Middle Byzantine Measles Ware vessels from Corinth. The American School of Classical Studies, Corinth Excavations, taken from *Corinth XI*, by C. Morgan

39 Middle Byzantine Slip Painted Ware vessels from Corinth. The American School of Classical Studies, Corinth Excavations, taken from *Corinth XI,* by C. Morgan

40 Middle Byzantine Slip Painted Ware jar from Corinth. The American School of Classical Studies, Corinth Excavations, taken from *Corinth XI*, by C. Morgan

41 Late Byzantine Slip Painted Ware plate in the Victoria and Albert Museum

42 Cypriot Sgraffito Ware vessel of Late Byzantine date, in the Victoria and Albert Museum

43 Middle Byzantine amphorae still lying in place in the shipwreck at Bozburun. Courtesy of the Institute of Nautical Archaeology

44 Elaborate Incised Ware. Close
   inspection of this vessel shows
   portions of yellow glaze beneath
   red-brown infilling of broad
   incisions. In the Victoria and
   Albert Museum

45 Elaborate Incised Ware. The dark infilling of
   the incisions cannot be explained by the
   combination of the overall glaze and the pale
   buff underlying fabric. It is clearly a deliberate
   decorative feature. In the Victoria and Albert
   Museum

46 Elaborate Incised Ware, also showing
   gouged incisions infilled with dark brown
   glaze, in the Victoria and Albert Museum

47 Incised Sgraffito Ware base sherd,
   probably from Istanbul

48 Late Byzantine Champleve Ware vessel from Corinth. The American School of
Classical Studies, Corinth Excavations, taken from *Corinth XI*, by C. Morgan

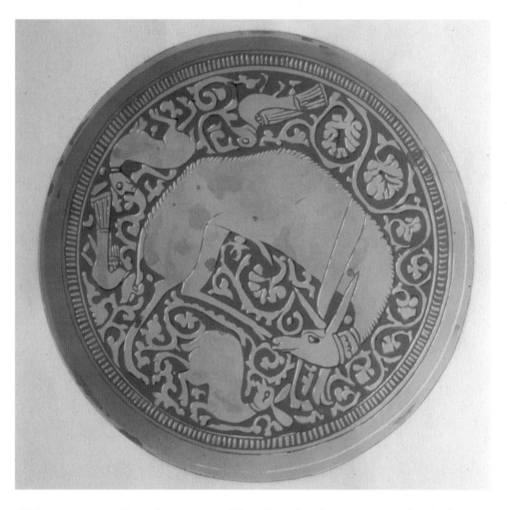

49 Late Byzantine Champleve Ware vessel from Corinth. The American School of
Classical Studies, Corinth Excavations, taken from *Corinth XI*, by C. Morgan

50 Late Byzantine Zeuxippus Ware, in the Victoria and Albert Museum

51 Stamped monogram on Late Byzantine vessel, in the Victoria and Albert Museum

52 Late Byzantine green glazed Incised Sgraffito Ware bowl, in the Victoria and Albert Museum

53 Late Byzantine yellow glazed Incised Sgraffito Ware bowl, in the Victoria and Albert Museum

54 Late Byzantine 'Thessaloniki Bird Bowl' variant of Incised Sgraffito Ware, showing characteristic rich yellow glaze and tripod marks, in the Victoria and Albert Museum

55 *Late Byzantine Green and Brown Painted Sgraffito Ware bowl, in the Victoria and Albert Museum*

56 *Late Byzantine Green and Brown Painted Sgraffito Ware bowl, in the Victoria and Albert Museum*

57 *Late Byzantine Coloured Sgraffito Ware bowl, in the Victoria and Albert Museum*

58 *Late Byzantine Coloured Sgraffito Ware goblet, in the Victoria and Albert Museum*

28 Middle Byzantine Fine Sgraffito Ware bowl, in the Victoria and Albert Museum

Islamic in addition to Byzantine techniques, one should not exclude the possibility of a closer connection with Polychrome Ware than is usually supposed.

The main fine-wares of the Byzantine Empire from *c.*700 to *c.*1000 were glazed whitewares but these were supplemented in the eleventh and twelfth centuries by a new range of products. These seem to emerge from yet another phase of experimentation and innovation.

New fine-wares in the eleventh and twelfth centuries

From the eleventh century onward a range of fine-wares in so-called 'red' (ranging from brick-red to pale buff) fabrics came into use. These could, at best, achieve an equally high standard of artistic and technical expertise as the earlier whitewares.[22]

The most important of these innovations for later developments in Byzantine pottery was the development of sgraffito decoration. This employs decorative designs scratched through the slip into the fabric. The first phase of Byzantine sgraffito-decorated pottery is characterized by the use of different colours of glaze on the interior and exterior of the same vessel. Such vessels — termed 'Duochrome Sgraffito Ware' by some scholars — characterize the eleventh century. This was rapidly succeeded in the twelfth century by vessels with a single, monochrome, glaze, almost always pale yellow or mid-green. These vessels are mostly shallow plates, bearing precisely carved decoration scratched into the 'red' body with a stylus, through a white or cream slip. The thin incisions are left unfilled, but show as darker lines against the paler slipped body. Such is the

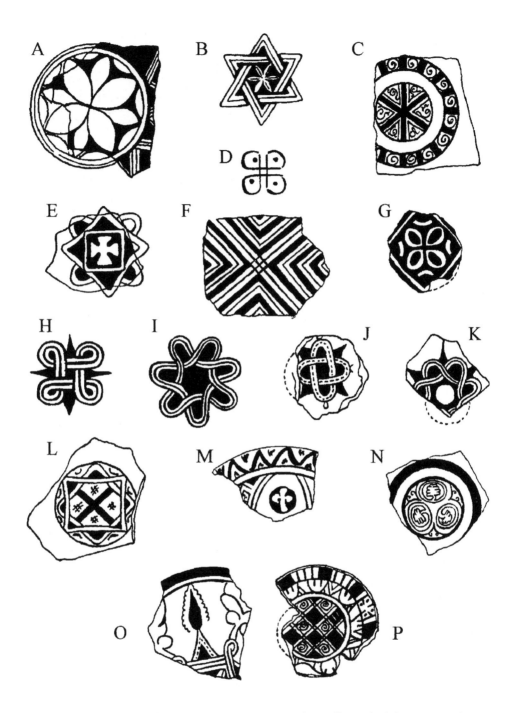

29 *Designs found on Middle and Late Byzantine Incised Sgraffito and Elaborate Incised Wares. B, E, H, K and L are variants of the 'interlace star' design widely used on this pottery. P is one variant of the common 'checkerboard' design.* After a drawing by David Talbot Rice, reproduced with the kind permission of the Talbot Rice family

30 Elaborate Incised Ware sherd showing the distinctive checkerboard design. From Istanbul

precision of the incisions that these monochrome sgraffito products have been termed 'Fine Sgraffito Ware'.

A division between 'Duochrome Sgraffito Ware' and 'Fine Sgraffito Ware' is difficult to sustain, as both are identical except for the exterior glaze colours. That is, 'Duochrome Sgraffito Ware' is nothing more than 'Fine Sgraffito Ware' with a different colour glaze on the exterior. It seems better to group these as a single class (called 'Fine Sgraffito Ware' here) in which eleventh-century examples had duochrome glaze while twelfth-century examples had a monochrome glaze.

The next development of Byzantine sgraffito pottery during the twelfth century was the use of broader incision. Instead of a stylus, a gouge was used to cut thick lines through the slip and expose areas of the fabric. This 'Incised Sgraffito Ware' began with vessels that resemble Fine Sgraffito Ware in their decoration, but employ a broader line. Soon, Incised Sgraffito vessels bore distinctive designs, such as those employing dot-in-circle motifs and radiating 'tendrils'. Among these distinctive groups of incised sgraffito pottery is one that is so widespread and distinctive to be widely studied as a separate class, Aegean Ware, well represented in shipwreck evidence.[23]

A 'luxury' version of Incised Sgraffito Ware is characterized by, often intricate, designs cut by gouge into the 'red' fabric through the pale slip and filled with darker glaze. This infill makes this immediately identifiable in relation to other sgraffito wares, and is a feature not found in earlier Islamic or Western pottery. It may have been a Byzantine innovation, and the finest examples are very 'elaborate'. It may justifiably be termed 'Elaborate Incised Ware', although in the past this has been employed for a much boarder range of ceramics, mostly lacking 'infilling' and so excluded from this class here.[24]

Charles Morgan noted the confusion generated by including a wider range of pottery in the original class of 'Elaborate Incised Ware'. Morgan observed that Talbot Rice's original category of 'Elaborate Incised Ware' encompassed Incised Sgraffito Ware, what is termed here Elaborate Incised Ware, Slip-Painted Ware and

Champleve Ware, whereas these are better separated as distinct classes. But this has, in turn, led some scholars (including Morgan) to overlook Elaborate Incised Ware, as defined here, as a distinct class of pottery.

This is more explicable in Morgan's case than in general, because the class is seemingly absent from Corinth. In fact, while Incised Sgraffito Ware is extremely widespread, Elaborate Incised Ware was apparently never very common. Definite examples of this latter class have only been found at Istanbul and Thessaloniki.

The defining characteristic of Elaborate Incised Ware is the infilling of incised designs. This is best seen on sherds where the dark infill can be seen to overlie another lighter layer of glaze within the incisions. That is, the class was produced by cutting the decoration into the fired clay through the slip, then covering the whole vessel with a green or yellow glaze, which was allowed to dry before painting the incisions with darker (usually dark brown) glaze and finally firing the whole vessel. The delicate painting with different coloured glaze is not specific to this class. It is found also on Petal Ware, where sometimes the 'petals' have alternating coloured dark and lighter glaze applied to them. This relationship may suggest an origin for the Elaborate Incised Ware before *c*.1200, although it is absent from Saraçhane and unlikely to have been common in the capital prior to that date.

In fact, the earliest dated examples of Elaborate Incised Ware come from the Great Palace of the Byzantine emperors at Istanbul. There, vessels of this class were associated with the final dated deposits, belonging to the twelfth century. The relevant sherds had a characteristic very pale yellow — almost transparent — glaze appearing almost white above a white slip. They include a small delicate bowl with a checkerboard of gilded squares in the interior and a gilded base, gilding in this case acting as the infill. This use of a 'white' effect produced by light yellow glaze over white slip is also found on the 'Constantine Bowl', today in The British Museum, which may belong to this class of pottery.[25]

31 The Constantine Bowl, showing checkerboard design on exterior, in The British Museum

The 'Constantine Bowl' is a hemispherical vessel with a checkerboard decoration 'inlaid' with blue in the thick white slip that covers the whole vessel, beneath a thin yellow lead glaze. Like the Great Palace sherds, it too appears 'white' at first sight and it seems possible that this is a deliberate effect. It may be that the white colour is in imitation of white-glazed Chinese or Islamic

32 Champleve Ware rim

pottery or of Polychrome Ware, which is also — unlike all other Byzantine pottery — gilded. Unlike the Great Palace sherds, the interior of the Constantine Bowl bears an incised depiction of Christ Pantocrator flanked by roundels containing coin-like portraits of Constantine the Great and Faustina (his first wife), identified by a Latin inscription around the interior near the rim. If genuine, as is apparently the case, it is by far the most artistically accomplished piece of Elaborate Incised Ware, and arguably the most artistically accomplished piece of Byzantine pottery, known.

So, a class of 'Elaborate Incised Ware', defined in this precise way, should be reinstated and its origin may bear some, albeit indirect, relation to Polychrome Ware. The skill involved in producing these vessels varies, but the finest examples and the scarcity of such pottery suggest that it was a luxury product. Its first appearance at the Great Palace in the twelfth century and limited distribution may imply a Constantinopolitan workshop, exporting perhaps only to Thessaloniki, the Empire's 'second city'.

Another twelfth-century innovation, Champleve Ware (in which portions of the slip are removed to show whole areas of the fabric below the glaze) may also be related to Incised Sgraffito Ware. This was probably made alongside both Incised Sgraffito Ware and Fine Sgraffito Ware from the twelfth century onward and widely used.

Champleve Ware was produced in the Constantinople/Thessaloniki/Athens fabric used for Fine Sgraffito Ware, although there is little direct evidence for its place(s) of manufacture. Both classes share similar decoration, such as pseudo-Kufic designs, hares and hunt scenes. The layout of decoration on both wares is also similar, although it is important to note that pseudo-Kufic symbols were already in use on Middle Byzantine whitewares and need attest no direct links with Islamic ceramics. Likewise, similar motifs also occur on Incised Sgraffito Ware vessels, implying a link between all these products.

These classes proved to be extremely long-lived, but in the twelfth century, alongside these other fine-wares, there seems to have been a shorter-lived fashion in southern Greece for red-painted, red-fabric glazed vessels. This included a range of classes, such as Imitation Lustre Ware, Spatter Painted Ware and Fingerprinted Ware, never commonly used even in Greece. They may well represent experimental products that were soon discontinued. Measles Ware was more commercially successful, but never as popular as those classes already mentioned.

Green and Brown Painted Ware proved much more successful than any of these red-painted wares. This too seems to have originated in the eleventh century, perhaps also in Greece, and was soon very widely used in most parts of the Byzantine Empire. It remained popular until and beyond the end of the Byzantine period. This rapid and sustained success is also shown by Slip Painted Ware, production of which appears to start in southern Greece (and perhaps Cyprus) in the eleventh century and be sustained for the rest of the Byzantine period and beyond.

Experimentation also included new production techniques. Until the eleventh century, glazed pots were stacked one on top of another when fired, as 'dribbles' of different coloured glaze on the exterior of pots indicate, but from the eleventh century 'kiln furniture' was used to separate pots. The earliest purpose-made 'kiln furniture' (dating to the eleventh century) comprises 'ox-yoke'-shaped clay separators, found for example at Corinth.

The eleventh and twelfth centuries were, therefore, a time of innovation for Byzantine potters. This phase of experimentation might be shorter than it at present appears, given the lack of chronological precision currently possible. It could belong, perhaps, to the end of the eleventh and the first half of the twelfth centuries.

Constantinople, and particularly Corinth, seem to have been the main centres for these innovations, a point reinforced as more pottery-manufacturing sites and larger quantities of Byzantine pottery are excavated and published. Prior to these discoveries one might have supposed that the publication of the Corinth material by Morgan and his successors had biased the picture, but it is increasingly apparent that he was, by chance, working on pottery from a, perhaps *the*, leading Byzantine centre of innovation in pottery decoration in the eleventh and twelfth centuries. However, it was not alone, as the development of Elaborate Incised Ware shows.

The innovations of the eleventh and twelfth centuries were to form the basis for all subsequent Byzantine fine-wares. These new products already played a central role in the Middle Byzantine ceramic tradition before the loss of most of the Empire to Westerners in the thirteenth century. When the production of whitewares ceased, these redwares — even Elaborate Incised Ware — were still manufactured.

It is possible that Byzantine sgraffito wares, Champleve Ware and Slip Painted Ware, while innovations in a Byzantine context, were copies of earlier pottery produced outside the Empire. Coloured sgraffito wares were developed in Mesopotamia from the ninth and tenth centuries. Byzantine sgraffito wares of the eleventh and twelfth centuries display several technical and artistic similarities with these. Moreover, Champleve and slip-painted wares were produced alongside these Mesopotamian sgraffito wares, as at Garrus.[26]

33 Middle Byzantine Fine Sgraffito sherd with pseudo-Kufic script as decoration, probably from Greece

This might suggest that Byzantine sgraffito wares, Champleve Ware and Slip-Painted Ware were imitations of these Mesopotamian products. This is often assumed to be the case, but the earliest Byzantine sgraffito ware — Fine Sgraffito Ware — is quite dissimilar to these 'Mesopotamian' products, not least because it has an unmixed glaze and no painted decoration to supplement this.

While there are several general similarities, more precise analogies for Byzantine products are also more difficult to find in this pottery than often realized. The sgraffito ware characteristic of northern Mesopotamia in the tenth to thirteenth century (Amol Ware) originated in the century before eleventh-century ('Duochrome') Fine Sgraffito Ware. This might suggest that Fine Sgraffito Ware was an attempt to copy Amol Ware, but although they both use a central hare motif, the Mesopotamian sgraffito ware with greatest similarity to the Byzantine products is not Amol Ware but Aghkand Ware, manufactured south-east of Tabiz.

However, Aghkand Ware is highly unlikely to have been the prototype for Byzantine Fine Sgraffito Ware, because it seems to date from the twelfth or thirteenth century. In particular, the production of Aghkand Ware with central figural roundels may only have begun *after* the currency of this design on Byzantine Fine Sgraffito Ware. So the link between Aghkand Ware and Byzantine Fine Sgraffito Ware cannot be one of Byzantine copying of an Islamic prototype. If a link exists between them, it is more likely that Aghkand Ware copied Byzantine Fine Sgraffito Ware.

This highlights a central problem regarding the origins and development of Byzantine sgraffito wares. Attempts to link the Mesopotamian and Byzantine ceramic innovations have been dominated by the assumption that the Islamic wares must have been the exemplars for Byzantine potters, rather than the opposite. Yet it is far from clear on archaeological grounds that this was the always the case.

However, there is no doubt that Byzantine potters also borrowed designs from the Islamic world during the ninth to twelfth centuries, as the use of pseudo-Kufic designs on Byzantine Polychrome Ware and Fine Sgraffito Ware shows. Pseudo-Kufic designs are copies of designs found in Islamic art based on the elaborate and stylized calligraphy (Kufic script) used in the Islamic world. The Byzantine use of these designs was simply as a decorative element, with the original meaning either not understood or deliberately denied by the reduction of letters to patterns.

How far Middle Byzantine potters had Islamic models, especially ceramics, from which to copy such designs is unclear. It is not at all clear that Islamic pottery was widely available in the eleventh- and twelfth-century Byzantine Empire. Few eleventh-century Mesopotamian sgraffito sherds have been found among thousands of sherds of Middle Byzantine pottery at Corinth, and at other sites the proportion of Islamic ceramics is equally low. The rarity of Islamic pottery from very large excavated assemblages of Middle Byzantine date from Istanbul implies that Mesopotamian pottery was not widely used there prior to the twelfth century. Although twelfth-century Islamic sherds were found at the Great Palace and Saraçhane, there is no hint that these were more than exotica at both sites. Mended vessels, with rivet holes reconnecting broken sherds, demonstrate that such pots were valued but this may also suggest that they were rare.[27]

Thus, the exact relationship between Mesopotamian and Byzantine sgraffito wares may be best understood as a two-way flow of technology and artistic concepts. Byzantine pottery drew on Islamic designs and Islamic potters may have borrowed designs from Byzantine potters: the case of the central figural roundel on Aghkand Ware may be a clear instance of this in practice.

There may also have been much less cultural 'content' to the production of sgraffito pottery than has often been supposed. Although sgraffito ware is often seen as characteristically Byzantine, their Islamic neighbours and Westerners (notably Italians) all made and used sgraffito wares after the eleventh century. The acceptability of Byzantine fine-ware pottery to Islamic tastes and Islamic fine-wares to Byzantines can be seen as paving the way for the next major stage of development in Byzantine fine-ware production, in which associations between pottery and particular political or religious identities weakened still further. This new stage of production was heralded by political events brought about by Western, not Islamic, interaction with the Byzantine Empire.

Conclusion

There were three main phases of Middle Byzantine fine-ware production. In the first, associated with the origins of glazed pottery in Europe and the Mediterranean, both red-wares and white-wares were manufactured. In the second, glazed white-wares (at finest, arguably, Polychrome Ware) seem to have been the main fine-wares in use. Finally, from the twelfth century, white-wares, provincial imitations of white-wares, sgraffito ware and Elaborate Incised Ware were used, supplemented by other — mostly painted — glazed products. The eleventh and twelfth centuries (perhaps only part of this period) were a phase of experimentation and innovation in Byzantine fine-ware, perhaps especially in Corinth. Middle Byzantine glazed pottery had a major effect on neighbouring ceramic traditions in Italy, the Balkans and the Islamic world. We should not assume the precedence of these in shaping innovations in Byzantine ceramic production.

The distinctive Middle Byzantine whitewares seem to have ceased to be made in the century following the capture of Constantinople in 1204 by the Fourth Crusade, and the establishment of the Latin Empire. Although parts of the former Empire remained under Byzantine rule, the majority passed into the hands of feudal western European landowners, with very different political, religious and cultural values to those of the Byzantine population who they ruled. This was to prove a relatively short transitional stage before a new range of fine-wares accompanied the Byzantine restoration in 1261.

Late Byzantine fine-wares

Again, just as the Early and Middle Byzantine periods have a distinctive ceramic 'signature', so too does the Late Byzantine period. In this case, this is provided by the use of a more restricted range of glazed pottery with cut- (sgraffito, champleve or incised) or slip-painted decoration. Plates are replaced by bowls as the most common form of fine-ware vessel, perhaps reflecting changes in dining customs, and this interpretation is supported by the disappearance of chafing dishes. Glazed ceramic tiles were no longer manufactured.

Late Byzantine glazes tend to be darker, more vitreous, and glossier than those of the Middle Byzantine period. The pale yellows and apple-greens of the Middle Byzantine period are replaced by dark — sometimes very dark — greens and (especially) a distinctive bright ochre or gold yellow. Red and polychrome painting ceases. Mottled glazes, of the sort found on Middle Byzantine whitewares, also disappear, while the combinations of several colours of glaze, mixed together or used as paint, become common. When designs are painted on, in glaze or slip, this usually disregards the cut designs of sgraffito wares.

Whereas Middle Byzantine fine-wares are both 'red-' and white-bodied, these later wares are exclusively 'red-bodied', although this term must again be taken to include red-buff, red-grey and even entirely buff-coloured fabrics. There seems to be visible variation between these 'red' fabrics, related to their origin.

In Thessaloniki, potters used a hard red fabric with white inclusions. In the north of Greece a soft orange/brick-red fabric was common and in western Anatolia a harder and redder fabric was employed — all contrasting with a southern Greek soft pinkish fabric. Specific kilns might also produce distinctive products: a characteristic class of Coloured Sgraffito Ware was produced at Serres in northern Greece (Serres Ware), distinguished both by its fabric and colouring. White clays, probably those used in the Middle Byzantine period, are found near Constantinople, in an area in imperial control until the fifteenth century. This

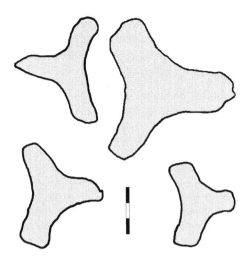

34 Outline shapes of tripods used for firing Late Byzantine pottery. Scale in cm. Based on a photograph by Papanikola-Bakirtzi

switch to 'red-bodied' wares may, therefore, have been an economic or even aesthetic choice, a point to which we shall return later.[28]

Technological change also renders Late Byzantine fine-wares distinct from Middle Byzantine products. 'Ox-yoke'-shaped clay separators were replaced in the thirteenth century by ceramic tripod stands, which left distinctive 'scars' (or 'tripod marks') on the interior of pots. Interestingly, no attempt seems to have been made to conceal or cover over these 'scars', even when they detract from the design of interior of a vessel.

Tripods were both hand-formed and mould-made, and their distinctive recti-linear or oval 'scars' are easily visible on the inner surface of pots. This is perhaps the most distinctive feature of thirteenth-century and later Byzantine pottery. Glaze droplets have been found on the rims of Byzantine pots bearing tripod 'scars' on their interior, implying that pottery was stacked upside down in the kiln, using the tripods as spacers. At some Late (and Post-) Byzantine kilns, such as Mikro Pisto in Thrace, wheel-made ceramic cones were also used to separate vessels during firing, but this may be a still later development and a chronological sequence of ox-yoke separators, tripods and cones may perhaps be discerned.[29]

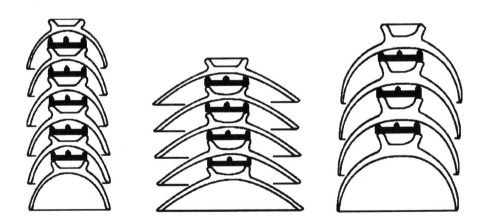

35 Diagram showing, in cross-section, the use of tripods in firing Late Byzantine pottery. After Papanikola-Bakirtzi

Incised Sgraffito Ware continued in production, although designs tend to be simpler and extend across the centre of vessels. These products include those referred to by some scholars as 'Plain Sgraffito Ware', but as the relevant vessels lack any unique defining features to warrant their separation into a distinct class, they are better seen as thirteenth-century and later Incised Sgraffito Ware with simple designs and very strongly coloured, usually ochre/golden yellow, glaze. Thus, what some scholars would term 'Plain Sgraffito Ware' is included in the class of 'Incised Sgraffito Ware' here, and taken to represent a Late Byzantine simplification of designs and greater standardization of colouring within this class of pottery.

Late Byzantine fine-wares comprised, therefore, a more restricted range of products, most of which have some superficial similarities to each other, manufactured in a new way. These co-existed with the circulation of much larger quantities of non-Byzantine imports than had hitherto been the case.

The importation of Italian ceramics, especially fine-wares, into the Late Byzantine Empire is very well attested and has already been described. Proto-Maiolica and other Italian wares, such as Veneto Ware and Ramina Manganese Rosso Ware, were all widely used in the Late Byzantine Empire. This trade was so extensive that at many Late Byzantine sites most fine-wares are of Italian origin. For example, at Arta 95 per cent of pottery in use during the Late Byzantine period was Italian.[30]

Even in rural contexts, Late Byzantine pottery was seldom immune to outside competition, as Italian imports indicate. For example, Italian pottery, including Proto-Maiolica, is found on rural Late Byzantine sites in the Peloponnese and in Crete. Western traders also brought smaller quantities of other products. For example, a fourteenth- or fifteenth-century Spanish bowl in a fine reddish-yellow fabric with white slip and purplish gold paint under coloured glaze, and bearing a Pseudo-Kufic design, has been found at Isthmia.

Islamic fine-wares were also imported into the Late Byzantine Empire, albeit to a lesser degree than Italian wares, and imitations of Islamic fine-wares were manufactured within imperial boundaries. For example, sherds of Rayy Ware have been identified at Istanbul and both Islamic pottery and imitations of Islamic pottery have been recognized at Corinth. The Late Byzantine Turquoise Glazed Ware produced in western Anatolia was probably an imitation of Rayy Ware, rather than representing a continuation of the earlier Syrian tradition of turquoise glazed pottery.[31]

Chinese ceramics are also more common in Late Byzantine contexts than is often supposed, although occur only in towns. One well-known variety of Chinese pottery, Celadon Ware, has been found at Ephesus, Sardis, Miletus and Antioch. Chinese pottery has also been found in thirteenth-century contexts at Corinth and at Istanbul. It was probably widely used, in small quantities, in Late Byzantine urban contexts.[32]

For the first time, Byzantine fine-ware producers had to compete with large quantities of imports, often of a higher technical quality. This begs the question of the origins of Late Byzantine products themselves and their cultural connections.

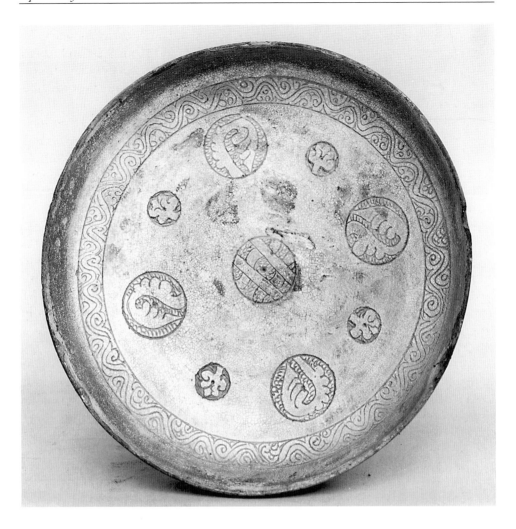

36 Middle Byzantine Incised Sgraffito Ware. Reproduced with the kind permission of The British Museum

The origins of Late Byzantine fine-wares

All the Byzantine fine-wares that became widespread after *c*.1200 relate to wider ceramic traditions than Middle Byzantine pottery alone. Similar fine-wares seem to have been produced elsewhere in the Balkans and in Italy. The Italian connections of both the Latin states and the Late Byzantine cities seem to have played an important role in shaping Late Byzantine tastes in ceramics. Some fine-wares were produced both in Byzantine territory and in the Crusader states of Palestine, such as St Symeon Ware. Through manufacture and trade a shared range of fine-wares came into use in the Late Byzantine Empire and parts of Italy, especially the Venice region (Veneto) of north-east Italy.[33]

Coloured sgraffito and Champleve wares were manufactured in Italy, the Crusader kingdoms, the Crimea and in Islamic areas. Zeuxippus Ware and copies of this class were produced in Italy, the Byzantine Empire and in the Crimea. Incised and slip-painted wares were produced in Byzantine contexts and elsewhere in the Balkans and the Crimea.[34]

It is clear, therefore, that Late Byzantine products were part of a common Mediterranean range of fine-wares. These seem to have carried few cultural associations, being acceptable in Christian and Islamic, Western and Byzantine, contexts alike. They catered for almost all the fine-ware needs of all these populations, although Chinese fine-wares were also used both by the Byzantines and, especially, their Islamic neighbours.

In Cyprus, the production of a distinctive local class of 'Late Byzantine' fine-ware — Cypriot Sgraffito Ware — seems to have broadly coincided with the loss of the island to Byzantine control at the end of the twelfth century. As this local variant of Coloured Sgraffito Ware developed from the Byzantine pottery tradition in the early thirteenth century, reflected ceramic fashions within the Empire and was manufactured by a formerly Byzantine population, it is usually counted as Byzantine. However, it is doubtful whether any Cypriot Sgraffito Ware was actually produced under Byzantine rule.

Late Byzantine fine-wares represent the last phase of Byzantine ceramic tradition before the fall of the Empire. They also outlived the Empire: the latest Coloured Sgraffito Ware, Incised Sgraffito Ware, Slip-Painted Ware (and possibly Late Turquoise Glazed Ware) were made long after 1453. These became the first Post-Byzantine pottery of Constantinople, Greece, the Balkans and Anatolia, and will be discussed in that context later. However, with no Byzantine Empire at all, such products cannot be termed Byzantine and are, therefore, outside the scope of this book, except in relation to the end of Late Byzantine fine-ware production.[35]

Conclusion

This summary shows that the three main phases of Byzantine political and cultural history have distinctive ceramic 'signatures' in terms of fine-ware pottery. This may imply that the conventional periodization of Byzantine history had some reality in the material circumstances of everyday life for people in the fifth to fifteenth centuries in the Byzantine world. Interestingly, broad trends seen in other aspects of Byzantine history are seen reflected in fine-wares. In the next chapter we will move beyond considerations of identification, dating, technology and origins to explore what pottery can tell us as a source for Byzantine society and economy.

4 The manufacture and marketing of Byzantine pottery

Introduction

In order to illustrate how pottery can be a valuable source for reconstructing the Byzantine world, this chapter will focus on pottery manufacture and trade. The next chapter will explore pottery as a source for Byzantine society and culture more widely. The exploration of these themes here will only touch on a few subjects for which ceramic evidence offers a useful source — much more could be said about all of them. However, the examples given here will illustrate the unexploited, but vast, potential of this plentiful — but usually overlooked — source for the Byzantine period.

The previous chapters show how pottery can elucidate technology and inter-cultural contacts, and also assist in archaeological dating. It is not my intention to pursue these further here, but it is worth noting that the revised chronologies for Byzantine and Italian pottery constructed by recent work, and hopefully the chronological revisions for Byzantine pottery suggested in this book, enable one to revise the published dating of many Byzantine sites.

In theory, ceramics could help to elucidate many of the broader questions about the Byzantine Empire. These questions include economic organization, the study of inter-regional links, art and its relation to society, religious history and the survival or decline of Classicism in the Byzantine period. Regrettably, some of the potentially most interesting ways in which pottery could help us to understand the Byzantine Empire are rendered impractical at present, at least for the Middle and Late Byzantine periods. Problems resulting from the variable recovery and erratic reporting of this material in the past have left much Byzantine pottery without a known archaeological context and render distributional studies very problematical.

For example, the lack of well-published, well-stratified and well-dated pottery from occupation sites inhibits spatial studies that could correlate pottery with specific buildings or activity-areas. This is impossible at most Middle and Late Byzantine sites. In order to achieve this, one would need much more extensive stratigraphical excavations published in sufficient detail as to enable pottery to be related to specific phases of particular structures and to areas outside any structure.

While Byzantine pottery can be used as an archaeological source, therefore, better recording and publication in future will enable a far wider range of topics to be explored using ceramic evidence. These include questions of social structure, the distribution of activities and the use of specific rooms within structures. It will be possible to plot changes in these across time and for the dynamics of settlements to be explored in much greater detail than is currently practical at the vast majority of Middle and Late Byzantine sites. Nevertheless, even with our currently flawed evidence for these periods, it is still possible to gain some valuable new information about the Byzantine Empire during these centuries from studying its pottery. Better recording and publication means that far more can be said about such questions using Early Byzantine material, but it would be very instructive to be able to compare this with evidence from later centuries. Even with flawed data such as these, one might hope that pottery would provide information about manufacture and trade in the Byzantine economy, and this is theme of this chapter.

The organization of Byzantine pottery production

Surprisingly little is known about the manufacturing sites used to produce Early Byzantine pottery, considering how much is known about the archaeology of other aspects of this period. Few large-scale excavations of the pottery-producing sites (including workshops and stores as well as kilns) belonging to the main red-slip ware producers of this date are published. It is impossible to comment on the general function, appearance and layout of such establishments in general. However, the scale of production and standardization of the products seen in these major 'industries' necessitates something beyond the level of what David Peacock has termed 'workshop' production.[1]

One possibility is that the largest-scale red-slip ware production operated on what has been termed by economists a 'proto-industrial' basis, where a regional cluster of producers operate together to manufacture a single product. This standardized product is then marketed on a regional or wider basis. Proto-industrialization does not involve factory-buildings or the application of technology to production methods. Instead, it depends upon traditional methods of manufacture, usually undertaken by dispersed workshops, with craftspeople working together to produce standardized products aimed at regional markets.[2]

Written evidence supports the view that organized production of this sort took place in the Early Byzantine Empire, although it does not directly refer to pottery production. Large 'manufactories' (*fabricae*) are known from textual sources to have undertaken large-scale and highly organized manufacturing, perhaps managed in an almost military style. Some had concentrations of workers under a single roof, although others were probably more dispersed and less regimented. Those that appear in texts are largely connected to official production, for military or bureaucratic requirements, not private commerce. But legal evidence shows that similar establishments were also in private hands in the sixth century.

That is, the concept of well-organized large-scale manufacture was present in both official and civilian circles in the Byzantine Empire when red-slip wares were being mass-produced. The scale of production evidenced by the products themselves suggests that the main producers of red-slip wares might well have been organized in this way. It is hard to see how estate-level producers or small workshops could have manufactured the quantities of red-slip wares found at Early Byzantine sites, or supplied the sustained long-distance trade required to supply distant markets, without the co-ordination of dispersed workshops.

However, red-slip ware production was probably an exception to otherwise small-scale pottery production in the Early Byzantine Empire. Local coarse-wares were apparently produced in much smaller establishments, analogous in size to modern Mediterranean village potteries, perhaps largely in villages and at monasteries. Excavated examples include Abu Mina in Egypt, where potting took place at an important pilgrimage centre, and Çiflik in Anatolia, where a coarse-ware kiln was situated close to an Early Byzantine church.[3]

An especially instructive coarse-ware kiln site, belonging to the seventh century, has been excavated at Dhiorios in Cyprus. There, a cluster of small rectangular buildings was associated with pottery production. Except for its date, this complex resembles many local workshops found throughout the Roman Empire, and may well be typical of the majority of rural workshops.[4]

The distances travelled overseas and the quantities of pottery involved, suggest that the red-slip wares were probably sold for profit, as part of well-organized long-distance trade (perhaps controlled though mercantile- or crafts-guilds). In contrast, the highly localised character of much coarse-ware manufacture suggests that this was often serving the needs of a specific village or monastery and organized on family or communal lines. However, some coarse-wares were traded long distances and it was worthwhile for the red-slip ware producers to manufacture their own coarse-wares. So it may be mistaken to assume that all workshops such as that at Dhiorios were wholly disengaged from the monetary economy and from market-based trade.

Another form of production may be discerned in relation to amphora manufacture. Analogy with the Roman period and direct evidence suggests that amphora kilns were closely linked to agriculture. This was principally because the goods exported in these vessels were usually wine, oil or foodstuffs. This close relationship between agriculture and amphorae is clearly seen in Early Byzantine Palestine, where 'Gaza' amphorae were used to transport Gaza wine. Indeed, the link may be more precisely between specialized agricultural production for export, than with agricultural activity in general. Thus, amphora production may have been at centres where such specialization occurred, in particular secular and monastic estates, rather than as part of subsistence agriculture. Consequently, amphora production may have taken place on a different basis to that of both red-slip ware and coarse-ware pottery, although these activities could also occur in close proximity on the same site.

Thus, although Early Byzantine fine-wares, coarse-ware vessels and amphorae could all be transported and traded together, they may result from different forms

37a Middle Byzantine kiln at Corinth. The American School of Classical Studies, Corinth Excavations, taken from *Corinth XI*, by C. Morgan

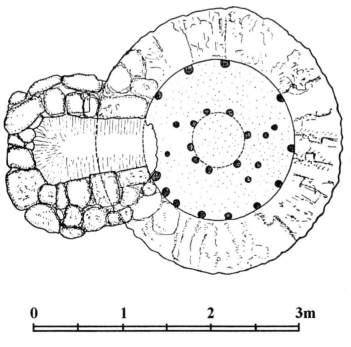

0   1   2   3m

37b Plan of Middle Byzantine kiln at Corinth shown in photograph above. The American School of Classical Studies, Corinth Excavations, taken from *Corinth XI*, by C. Morgan

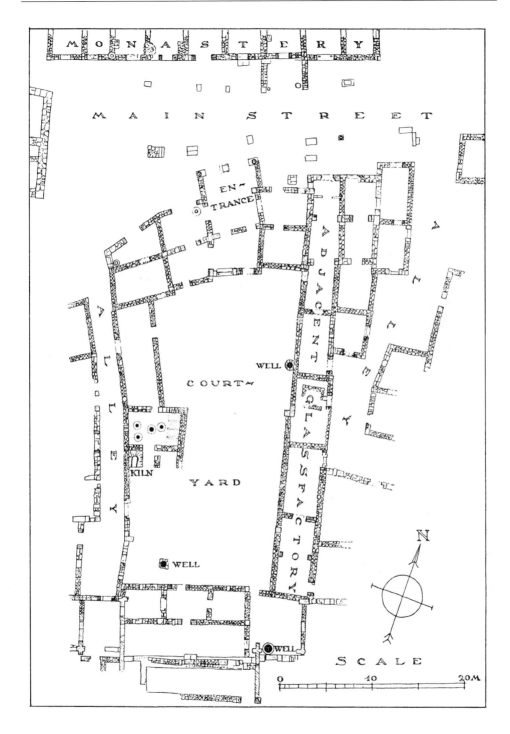

38 Middle Byzantine pottery- and glass-making establishments at Corinth. The American
School of Classical Studies, Corinth Excavations taken from *Corinth XI*, by C.
Morgan

of production. Only red-slip ware production may have been primarily designed to provide vessels for market-based long-distance trade. Local coarse-ware production primarily fulfilled local needs, although these vessels too were sometimes traded more widely. Amphora production was probably a by-product of the need to transport and store goods (especially the results of specialised production) for trade. As such, only red-slip ware production may have been undertaken by full-time commercial firms manufacturing pottery for wider markets with the aim of regaining profits principally through coin.

There is no hint that proto-industrial manufacture of fine-wares (if this is what we see in the case of the Early Byzantine red-slip wares) survived the cessation of Early Byzantine fine-ware production in the seventh century. All Middle Byzantine pottery could have been produced in small-scale workshops or on an estate-basis, as had Early Byzantine coarse-wares and amphorae. The twelfth-century writer Balsamon considered potteries to be part of agricultural property and this is what we would expect in relation to the coarse-wares (including the amphorae), given the evidence from the vessels themselves of widespread continuity from the Early Byzantine period.[5]

However, by the end of the Middle Byzantine period, pottery workshops could be substantial complexes, beyond the scale of 'village potteries'. Perhaps

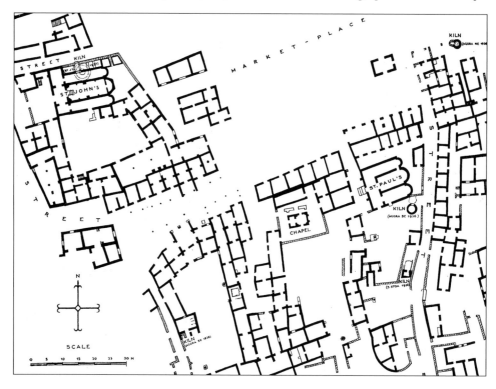

39 Pottery kilns amid churches and houses, Middle Byzantine Corinth. American School of Classical Studies, Corinth Excavations, taken from *Corinth XI*, by C. Morgan

the best evidence for large Middle Byzantine pottery workshops of this sort comes from Corinth, where a complete establishment of the late eleventh and twelfth centuries was excavated. This comprised a courtyard surrounded by stone-built rectangular rooms and served by wells. In the centre of one side was a kiln and manufacturing area, while on the opposite side of the courtyard was a glass-works.[6]

Another similar Middle Byzantine pottery workshop was also excavated at Corinth, near the Agora and adjacent to the Byzantine church of St Paul. This also comprised a courtyard surrounded by rectangular buildings and containing kilns and wells. These two complexes, and other less complete archaeological evidence from elsewhere, give a very clear picture of pottery-making in Corinth towards the end of the Middle Byzantine period. This suggests workshops catering both for local communities and producing vessels for more distant trade.

Elsewhere, evidence for Middle Byzantine pottery production is much less complete. For example, no kiln site producing Middle Byzantine whitewares has been excavated and written sources do not refer at all to pottery production in Constantinople. Judith Herrin has drawn attention to textual evidence that potters were brought from Greece in the eighth century to assist with the repair of the capital's aqueducts. This might suggest that potting was absent from the City, although perhaps specialists in hydraulic ceramics were required. Herrin has also pointed out that no potters are mentioned in the twelfth-century *Book of the Eparch*, a tract regulating trades in Constantinople.[7]

The anomaly between the written sources and archaeological evidence for pottery production in Constantinople may be explained if pottery production was somehow subsumed in other activities taking place in the capital. One possibility is of a continuing association between pottery production and monasteries, first visible in the Early Byzantine period. At the great monastic centre at Mount Athos, the Lavra monastery bought a potter's workshop near the sea in 952, and in 982 the monastery of Iveron also had a pottery by the sea. The coastal location of the kilns might imply that production was for export rather than for the monasteries' own requirements but whether or not this was the case, this could be taken to suggest that monasteries might be one possible location for potteries in the Byzantine capital. If pottery-production took place in monastic contexts this might well have escaped special notice.[8]

The existence of urban kilns seems very likely on comparative grounds also. Archaeological evidence suggests that urban potteries were widespread. There were even kilns at small towns such as Oreoi, Greece, where Fine Sgraffito Ware was produced in the eleventh and twelfth centuries. However, not all Middle Byzantine pottery production was urban-based, as we see for example at Ganos on the Black Sea coast of Anatolia.[9]

It is, therefore, possible that textual sources do not mention whiteware production in Middle Byzantine Constantinople because this took place in monasteries or other institutions, or that it was in some way connected to such communities. This may be supported by the discovery of whiteware wasters at two

40 Bottom of glazed Byzantine bowl, showing brown glaze over light coloured slip above fabric, in the Victoria and Albert Museum

Constantinopolitan church sites, and a whiteware waster from the Great Palace may suggest that pottery production was also subsumed in court life.[10]

The production of whitewares inside the Great Palace may also be implied by the production of imitations in courtly contexts in Bulgaria. The way in which Polychrome Ware tiles were produced in the Bulgarian court may give us a glimpse of how their manufacture took place in the Byzantine capital. Kilns found adjacent to the Bulgarian royal sites and monasteries at Preslav, Patleina, Tuzlaluka and Selishte producing Polychrome Ware copies had workshops laid out in a chain-like pattern representing stages of production. At Tuzlaluka, four rooms were used in sequence for forming the tile, painting the formed tile using mineral pigment or metal oxides, covering the painted decoration with glaze, and — lastly — for firing to fix the decoration and glaze.[11]

Although organized in the same systematic way, each workshop apparently specialized in particular versions of this ceramic, while sharing common motifs. This form of highly organized production, if based on a Byzantine model, suggests that from the outset the manufacture of these tiles was meticulously regulated. Production of Polychrome Ware tiles at Preslav seems to have been contemporary with the establishment of the town as the Bulgarian capital in AD 893. If borrowed from the Byzantine court before 893, systematic production in this way could have been established when Basil 1 used similar tiles in the Great Palace in the 860s-80s, if not before.

In the eleventh and twelfth centuries there is more evidence for substantial urban-based pottery production. This may be associated with the phase of innovation evidenced by the appearance of new classes of 'red' fabric fine-ware. Fine-ware production seems only to have become common outside Constantinople at this time, and this may be associated with these organizational changes in pottery production.[12]

However, there is little trace of any technological change in pottery production prior to the eleventh century. Wheel-marks show that all Byzantine fine-wares were wheel-turned, whatever their date. This is also true for most coarse-wares, which often have more pronounced wheel-marks. The permanent kilns known from sites in Greece, Cyprus, the Balkans and the Crimea show little change from the fifth to twelfth centuries. They are mostly domed cylindrical structures with fire-pits beneath the chamber, although there were also rectangular kilns. In rectangular kilns, the superstructure was arched, while it was domed in the curvilinear examples. These kilns used the 'updraft method', where unfired vessels were stood on a perforated clay floor within the kiln and wood added through an opening below the floor to provide fuel.[13]

Pamela Armstrong has argued that there were no major changes in Byzantine glazing technology from the ninth to thirteenth centuries. She suggests firing temperatures ranging between *c*.900-1000 degrees C and it has independently been suggested that Middle Byzantine Polychrome Ware tiles were fired at 750-850 degrees C. Likewise, throughout this period (and later) the Byzantines only used lead glazes, comprising lead- and silica-oxides prepared in fired clay crucibles and painted onto the pottery. Lead glazes were coloured by adding iron for red, copper for green, manganese for purple, with yellow and brown probably produced by varying the amount of iron added to the glaze. Adding less than one per cent iron would give yellow, whereas two or three per cent iron gave brown. Lead and other minerals were also used to colour paint.

Occasionally, direct evidence for the composition of designs can be identified on Middle Byzantine pottery. For example, traces of holes caused by the compass used to draw out geometric patterns have been found on Middle Byzantine Polychrome Ware and Fine Sgraffito Ware sherds.

In addition to kiln sites, wasters also hint at several sgraffito ware production sites. For example, Guy Sanders has noted Fine Sgraffito Ware and Aegean Ware wasters at Sparta implying a twelfth-century pottery workshop at or near the Hadrianic Stoa. There is another (previously unpublished) Fine Sgraffito Ware waster from the theatre at Sparta in the Victoria and Albert Museum in London.[14]

Late Byzantine pottery manufacturing is poorly understood, although texts imply rural production beyond the immediate needs of village communities. For example, in 1316 the village of Radolibos had seven potteries. Only a few kilns are known, as at Serres and Thessaloniki. Some scholars have employed 'ethno-archaeology' (the observation and recording of modern activities) to reconstruct the details of manufacture, studying traditional Greek and Cypriot potteries which they believe preserve Late Byzantine technology and manufacturing practices. On this basis, it has been suggested that clay for potting was first pounded with a large wooden mallet and then sieved, before being placed in a wooden tank to permit the unwanted components to separate. This would then be drained and the pure clay dried in the sun before throwing the vessel on a foot-driven wheel. Such a reconstruction of Late Byzantine pottery-making practice is credible in general terms, but technological innovations may have occurred, or technology may have been lost, between the Byzantine period and the period when ethnographic observations were made.[15]

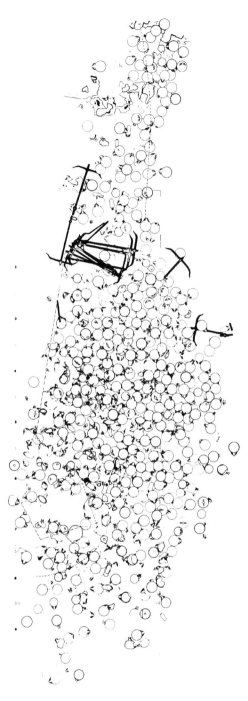

41 Plan of the Early Byzantine shipwreck at Yassı Ada II, showing amphora in position in its hold. Courtesy of the Institute of Nautical Archaeology

Regional differences in production methods may also have varied, with different methods used for different products. Such limitations suggest that ethnographic evidence should only be used with caution, and as a general indication of possible production methods. In support of such an approach, Charles Morgan described mid-twentieth-century Greek traditional potteries closely resembling the plan of Middle Byzantine potteries at Corinth.[16]

This forces us to look at Late Byzantine pottery itself for indications of how production was organized. Late Byzantine fine-wares are harder fired and often more thinly potted than Middle Byzantine products. They frequently have 'cleaner' clay, rendering a fabric with fewer inclusions. This is especially true of Zeuxippus Ware, which was produced to a very high technical standard. Glazes seem also to show technological improvements, while the use of tripods might have increased the rate of production. This may suggest increased output on the part of many small-scale potteries, competing with Western imports by improvements in manufacturing techniques.

Consequently, from the fifth to the thirteenth centuries the manufacture of Byzantine pottery can be seen to change according to the wider context of the Byzantine Empire. In particular, the seventh century as a period of economic crisis and the eleventh and twelfth centuries periods of urban renewal are clearly seen to correlate with probable shifts in the organization of pottery production. These patterns can also be detected when we examine the ceramic evidence for Byzantine trade.

Pottery and trade in the Byzantine economy

Pottery obviously affords a potential means of studying trade and, in the Byzantine case, of how trading patterns changed over 1000 years. Early Byzantine fine-wares and amphorae have been often been discussed in this context, especially in relation to 'the end of the Ancient Economy' in the seventh century. However, there has been surprisingly little work aiming to reconstruct Middle and Late Byzantine trade, especially trading networks within the Empire, through the study of pottery.[17]

The fastest mode of bulk transport in the Byzantine Empire was almost always by sea and, therefore, most long-distance trade was by sailing ship. Technologies of ship-building were advanced enough to have produced efficient sea-going trading-ships long before the fifth century AD. A series of shipwreck sites from the fourth century AD onward show that a high standard of ship design, derived from Roman ship-building techniques, was maintained until the twelfth century. Archaeological and textual sources both attest the vitality of sea-borne trade throughout the Early Byzantine period. Although most Early Byzantine trading ships known from ship-wrecks were smaller than their earlier Roman counterparts, these were still large enough to carry substantial cargoes of amphorae — the wreck at Agios Stephanos yielded over 1000 Byzantine amphorae in an area of 24 x 12m.[18]

From the fifth century onward, most of the major centres of the Empire, including the capital Constantinople, were provided with harbours suitable for such vessels. At these ports, warehouses and dock facilities enabled bulk cargoes to be handled and distributed to local retailers. The market provided by such urban centres in the Early Byzantine period combined with the capacity for sea-transport to produce regular and intensive long-range trade. Exploitation of this Empire-wide market began before the fifth century and continued, although changing in character and scale, while the Mediterranean was safe for traders, throughout the Early Byzantine period.

In the fifth to seventh centuries, this trade was in the hands of professional merchants and ship-owners based in the major towns of the Empire. These acted both independently and as part of trading guilds or associations. Trading networks established by such merchants linked the coastal areas of the Empire and extended far beyond.

There is extensive evidence — including ARSW in Constantinople and Egyptian Painted Ware in Palestine — for trade in fine-ware pottery within the Empire. Many shipwreck sites around the Mediterranean demonstrate bulk trade in wine, oil and other goods carried in amphorae. There are even mosaic depictions of trading ships and amphorae, such as that from the 'House of Kyrios Leontis Kloubas'at Scythopolis (Beth Shean in modern Israel) where Palestinian amphorae are depicted on the deck of a fifth-century sailing ship. As Sean Kingsley has pointed out, care was even taken to show the main fabric colours of the amphorae.[19]

Shipwrecks show that vessels seldom carried a single class of amphora, even if these held only one product. For instance, at Iskandil Burnu, Turkey, a later sixth- or seventh-century ship measuring at least 18 x 4m contained Palestinian, Gazan and Egyptian amphorae — all probably for wine. This pattern of mixed amphorae (although not always the same combination) is typical of Early Byzantine shipwreck sites. However, six shipwrecks from Dor and that at Gigat Olga, Israel, demonstrate the regional popularity of specific classes (in this case Palestinian amphorae) closer to their place of manufacture. Likewise, old amphorae might be reused, and taken back to be refilled.

Amphorae (that is to say, their contents) are generally the main cargo found at shipwreck sites but fine-wares and glass vessels (most likely in wooden crates) were used as high-value 'space-fillers'. A mixed cargo of wine, oil and other commodities in amphorae could be supplemented by fine-ware pottery. Perishable materials such as textiles or leather goods might also have been traded, which would leave little trace at most archaeological sites.

Amphorae and secondary cargoes were carried both on and below deck, with holds packed tightly with vessels. At Dor Wreck J, dendrochronologically dated AD 415-530 but perhaps wrecked in the late sixth or seventh century, it is even possible to show that the amphorae may have been linked by loops of rope over their necks and held in place during transit by padding. It is possible that the characteristic grooving of Early Byzantine amphorae was to facilitate the grip of such ropes, as well as that of the cargo-handlers in port.

Shipwrecks show that amphorae were stopped with a pottery disk or bung, held in place by resin or pitch, and often also lined with pitch when carrying wine. In addition to the goods in transit, wrecks often provide evidence of the vessels used by crews, found together in the cabin area. These may help us to date the ship and its cargo if dendrochronological dating is unavailable, and show how combinations of vessels were used together. 'Cabin' assemblages, like the composition of cargoes, also elucidate the origin of the ship, given the regionalism of Early Byzantine ceramics.[20]

The duration and number of trips possible for each ship in a year were hindered by practical considerations. Sailing-seasons were limited by the weather and by law (the Theodosian Code restricted maritime trade to between 13 April and 15 October) and the maximum speed of trading ships was possibly no more than six knots. Within these restrictions, Early Byzantine traders operated throughout the Mediterranean and far beyond the borders of the Empire.[21]

Pottery may give a clear indication of the distribution and character of Early Byzantine sea-borne trade beyond the frontiers of the Empire in the West. Byzantine pottery is found in Italy, Spain, France, Britain and even Ireland. Interestingly, a similar trade also seems to have taken place to the East and South, taking Early Byzantine ceramics down the North African coast, and especially to the Crimea, an area which was partly within the Empire.[22]

The intensity of trade may also be indicated by shipwreck and ceramic evidence. Trade may well have greatly increased in the fifth and sixth centuries, to judge from the relative proportions of shipwrecks of different dates in the Mediterranean and the quantity of traded ceramics found. For example, off the coast of Israel, twice as many Early Byzantine shipwrecks occur as for *any* previous period.[23]

42 Byzantine glazed bowl from shipwreck, showing characteristic encrustation from long submergence, in the Victoria and Albert Museum

Trade with the West seems to have had a distinctive organization. In fifth- to seventh-century western Europe, Byzantine mercantile communities were resident in political and ecclesiastical foci and in towns such as Marseilles and Bordeaux along trade routes inland. These communities maintained a Byzantine way of life, owned property and had their own churches.[24]

These Byzantine 'mercantile communities' appear also to have served official functions for the Byzantine imperial government, acting as embassies or imperial agents, and their activities were subject to regulation by the Byzantine authorities. Less formally, the religious and professional associations of merchants offered a connection between the eastern Mediterranean and western Europe, and the existence of these communities fulfilled both diplomatic and trading purposes.

Consequently, Byzantine mercantile communities in the West formed a vital, but frequently overlooked, link between western Europe and the Early Byzantine world. This link brought Westerners directly into contact with people from a society in which far more remained of the Late Roman past than was the case in many Western contexts. It gave them access to news and information about the Byzantine Empire from some of its most widely-travelled inhabitants and enabled access to specifically Mediterranean products.

This East-West trade route co-existed with a north-south trade route between western Europe and North Africa. The latter was probably differently organized and not wholly under Byzantine control. These two systems accounted for almost all of western Europe's fifth- to seventh-century overseas trade and formed an important routeway for new beliefs and cultural practices to enter the West.

In fact, the largest assemblage of such pottery outside the Mediterranean occurs at the rocky eroded coastal headland at Tintagel in Cornwall. There, ARSW, PRSW and a range of Byzantine amphorae are associated with what may be a royal fortress of fifth- to seventh-century date. This was in an independent British kingdom far to the west of the part of Britain under 'Anglo-Saxon' political control. The finds also include ceramic stoppers from amphorae, indicating that at least some probably arrived at the site still-sealed, and Byzantine coarse-wares. The possibility that the latter indicates the presence of Byzantine merchants at the site — a substantial settlement probably containing over 100 buildings — is enhanced by the discovery there of ship's water jars of Byzantine form.

If so, this may be the best candidate from Britain for a Byzantine mercantile community of the sort attested in Gaul, Spain and Italy. Interestingly, that possibility is further supported by Anne Bowman's demonstration that sailing times from the eastern Mediterranean to Britain would probably have precluded trade for profit alone. This suggests the possibility of Byzantine traders fulfilling a diplomatic as well as an economic function at the site.

The links established by these mercantile communities might, therefore, have extended across most of Europe in the later fifth and sixth centuries. But neither Byzantine ceramic imports nor Byzantine mercantile communities are evidenced in the West after the seventh century. Information from pottery about the trade networks of the Byzantine Empire in the eighth century is scarce, partly due to the difficulty in identifying eighth-century material. No Middle Byzantine shipwreck containing whitewares has been published (although a ninth-century shipwreck containing whiteware is said to have been identified), and around the Black Sea shipwreck evidence and amphorae suggest an interruption of seaborne trade from the seventh to eleventh centuries.[25]

This seems borne out by terrestrial pottery distributions. Byzantine white-wares of the eighth to tenth centuries are found largely within the Empire, rather than beyond its borders to the West. There is no evidence of Byzantine merchants providing such fine-wares to Western markets, and Middle Byzantine ceramics of other sorts, including amphorae, are extremely rare in the West, even in Italy. Trade was clearly reorganized after the seventh century, and cargoes mostly shipped between Constantinople and the other ports of the Empire in the seventh to eleventh centuries, not beyond the imperial frontiers.

This pattern alters again in the eleventh and twelfth centuries, when trade appears to 'internationalize' once more. Shipwreck sites become more common, as for example at Peristera in the north Sporades, where the ship carried a cargo of amphorae. Eleventh-century shipwrecks are especially common in the Aegean, and finds from these wrecks suggest that cargoes comprised of fine-wares and amphorae (at least 1500 vessels are known from one shipwreck site) were being shipped across political, religious and geographical frontiers to supply distant markets at this time.[26]

For example, at Serçe Limani an eleventh-century shipwreck contained both Islamic fine-wares and Byzantine amphorae. In this case, the ship's crew were probably Bulgarian or Byzantine Christians — pig-bones (pork being forbidden to both Jews and Muslims) and Greek Christian graffiti were found in the ship. This new 'internationalization' of trade is implied by other shipwrecks. For example, the Selimye shipwreck, off the Anatolian coast, contained a cargo of ninth- or tenth-century amphorae with its closest parallels in the Crimea.

43 Late Byzantine Aegean Ware. Reproduced with the kind permission of The British Museum

Some ships seem to have carried fine-wares as one of their principal cargoes. This evidence for bulk trade in fine-wares coincides with the emergence of larger scale urban potteries, perhaps capable of supplying more extensive markets. The characteristic redware products of these potteries are found at shipwreck sites, strengthening the case for an association between these patterns.

Guy Sanders has pointed out that excavated evidence suggests that decorated glazed pottery becomes common at Sparta, Thebes and Athens only in the twelfth century and may have become widespread in the countryside during that century also. It is possible that the increased availability of these fine-wares represents the terrestrial counterpart of this maritime archaeological pattern.[27]

The pattern of increased scale of production, the shipping of bulk cargoes of fine-ware and the more widespread use of glazed pottery, may result from wider changes in the Byzantine economy in the eleventh and twelfth centuries. The growth of towns, seen at Corinth and Pergamon, may have created new markets for 'everyday luxuries' such as highly decorated glazed fine-ware. If so, shipping fine-wares around the Empire might have become profitable once again, as these new markets expanded.

From the thirteenth century throughout the Late Byzantine period, a trading network centred on north-east Italy brought a standardised series of products, including pottery, to Byzantine and non-Byzantine areas of the eastern Mediterranean alike. We can see this most clearly in relation to Zeuxippus Ware, common both in thirteenth-century northern Italy and in the eastern Mediterranean on Byzantine and non-Byzantine (but not Islamic) sites.

In the Late Byzantine period too, recognizably Byzantine shipwrecks become rare once again, perhaps as trade passed increasingly into the hands of Italian merchants. Despite this, the thirteenth-century wrecks at Kastellorizo (east of Rhodes) and Skopelos contained cargoes of Incised Sgraffito Ware, along with lesser quantities of other fine-wares. This could well imply that the trade in fine-wares established in the twelfth century survived into the thirteenth century and that it was still supplied by Byzantine producers.

Cargoes stored in amphorae were still carried by Byzantine vessels into the thirteenth century. The shipwreck excavated at Çamalti Burnu contained a cargo of thirteenth-century amphorae of Günsenin types IV and III, with Greek monograms on the shoulder. The Çamalti Burnu shipwreck might legitimately be taken as symbolizing the very last phase of the Byzantine amphora trade, as Günsenin has suggested. But by *c*.1400 this was displaced by Italian vessels carrying wine and other goods in barrels, not amphorae.[28]

Monograms on Byzantine pottery: commerce or pilgrimage?

At first sight it might seem that another informative source of evidence for trade is the use of stamped or painted monograms on twelfth- and thirteenth-century fine-wares and amphorae. A few amphorae of this date carry painted inscriptions referring to their contents, such as beans or rice. Stamps showing monograms or depictions of animals or geometrical shapes are more common, especially after the twelfth century. A bronze die found at the Synaxis monastery in Thrace may well have been used to produce such impressions. Stamped monograms, comprising one or two Greek letters, also occur on other Byzantine vessels from the twelfth century onward. These were placed where most easily visible, in the central roundel of the bases of bowls.[29]

No systematic survey of these Middle Byzantine pottery stamps or monograms has been accomplished since the 1930s, but the same monograms occur on numerous vessels and they were added during manufacture. This highlights the problem of their meaning.

All the letters used could refer to Byzantine personal names. There are fewer than a dozen common monograms found on fine-wares and these occur widely in the Byzantine world on a minority of broadly contemporary vessels. The most commonly found are, perhaps, G (for Georgios), K (for Konstantinos), MI (for Michael) and P (for Phillipos). That the monograms indicate personal names seems to be borne out by rare vessels actually bearing names, such as Georgios, and is the most credible explanation for this practice. Several of these names were those of Byzantine emperors and it has been suggested that one vessel from Istanbul bears the monogram of the Palaeologan dynasty, but an imperial explanation does not seem to account for all the monograms.

Alternatively, the small range of monograms known might be taken to suggest that they represent different potters or 'firms' producing the pots. However, only a small proportion of Byzantine fine-ware vessels seem to have had monograms placed on them,

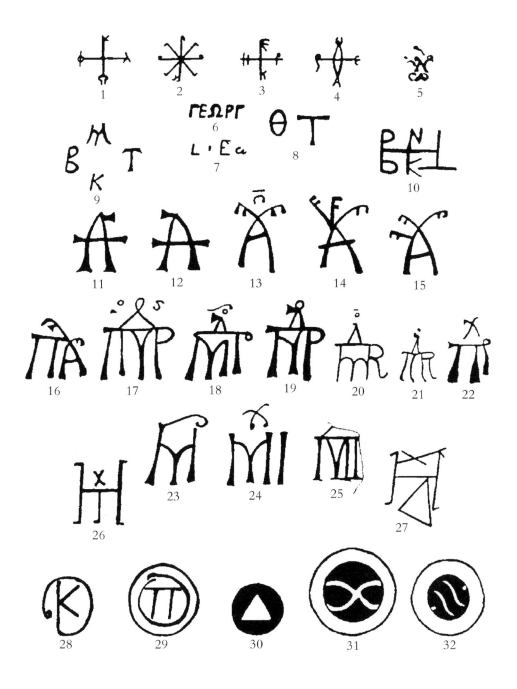

44 Monograms found on Late Byzantine pottery. 3, 5, 9, 11-12, 14, 16, 18-19, 21-25, 28, 30-2 are from Istanbul. 4 and 7 are from Thessaloniki. 6, 15, and 26-7 are from the Crimea. The remainder are unprovenanced. By David Talbot Rice, reproduced with the kind permission of the Talbot Rice family

so they are unlikely to be 'trade-marks'. For example, at the Mangana site in Istanbul, only two or three types of monogram can be recognized among hundreds of sherds.

Moreover, no one monogram is especially common in any one part of the Empire, as one might expect if they represented manufacturers-marks. The K, G and MI monograms occur in Constantinople, Thessaloniki, Ephesus and Cyprus, but always on only a small number of vessels. They also occur on a wide range of products, including Elaborate Incised Ware, Incised Sgraffito Ware, Slip-Painted Ware and Zeuxippus Ware. So, there is no clear correlation between monograms and geographical locality, or between monograms and classes of pottery.

Although letters were used by the Byzantines to specify quantity, as on Byzantine bronze coinage, there is no evidence that the monograms correlate with specific sizes or shapes of vessel. Sometimes the volume of vessels bearing similar monograms, when reconstructable, would be drastically different. For example, identical monograms occur on both large plates and small cups.

A more credible interpretation may be found if we compare these monograms with the religious symbols found on Middle Byzantine whitewares. These are also in the centre of the vessels on which they are found and, like the monograms, may be either stamped or painted. If so, these monograms might well designate saints' names, such as St Michael and St Constantine (as suggested by Demetra Papanikola-Bakirtzi), rather than manufacturers, places of manufacture or details relating to the use of the vessel. This would at least explain why the same monograms occur on different classes of pottery, produced in different parts of the Empire but always on a minority of pots.[30]

Papanikola-Bakirtzi has suggested that this could be related to pilgrimage, with stamped vessels acquired at pilgrimage centres. This may also explain their occurrence in greater numbers than usual at the excavations of the Mangana, an important monastery in Constantinople. If the Palaeologan dynastic monogram in fact occurs on one such vessel, perhaps this was felt appropriate in a religious context given the claimed sanctity of the imperial court.

The use of monograms may, therefore, be a less useful source for reconstructing trading patterns that might initially be hoped. Nevertheless, Greek monograms might help us to distinguish Byzantine from non-Byzantine products at a period when many classes of fine-ware crossed 'national' borders. The occurrence of monograms on Zeuxippus Ware may be significant in this context. Monogrammed vessels might even eventually be used to elucidate patterns of pilgrimage, if one assumes that pilgrims brought them back to their home communities. This brings us to the relationship between pottery and Byzantine culture, a topic insufficiently explored in most published work on this material.

5 Ceramics as a source for reconstructing Byzantine culture

Introduction

It is reasonable to assume that pottery might tell us something of the everyday life of the Byzantine population and how this changed over time. There are several ways in which ceramics relate to daily life. The most obvious relationship between pottery and daily life is the use to which pottery was put in everyday activities.

We have seen that cooking pots changed little over the Byzantine period. Between the fifth and twelfth centuries there were few changes in the range of these vessels and, therefore, perhaps the cooking practices associated with them remained equally unchanged. Cooking pots with their bases blackened from burning show that these were placed directly over an open fire. Double-handled vessels imply that they were lifted to and from the fire with both hands and the lack of flat bases may imply that they were not set directly onto the table. Food was then presumably taken from the cooking-pot and placed into other vessels for consumption.

We have direct evidence of the forms that these other vessels took. In the Early Byzantine period, food was probably often eaten from red-slip ware and painted

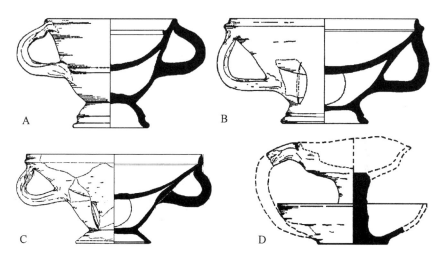

45 Examples of forms of Middle Byzantine Glazed Constantinopolitan Whiteware chafing dishes (A-C) and a lamp (D), from Istanbul. After Peschlow *et al.*

fine-ware plates and bowls. Wine was the most likely drink accompanying this, again apparently decanted from amphorae into jugs to serve at the table. This may imply that preparation for meals took place away from the dining table, perhaps in a designated 'kitchen' area. Interestingly, glass vessels are commonly found even in low-status houses at this period and glasses probably served along with pottery cups as everyday drinking vessels for wine.[1]

These eating practices changed after the seventh century, when handled pottery cups, 'fruit stands' and chafing dishes appear. The increased use of pottery cups may reflect a decline in the use of glass at the table, perhaps due to the better ability of glazed pottery for holding liquid. The use of 'fruit stands' and chafing dishes suggests the careful presentation of food. This may also suggest that food was kept warm at the table, implying longer, or at least differently 'structured', meals in which more than one dish was served at each sitting. One vessel from Corinth may imply that the contents of chafing dishes could contain liquid, such as gravy or sauce, as perhaps is depicted in glaze as dripping down the outside of the vessel![2]

After *c.*1200, cooking vessels shaped like frying pans become almost the only shapes at many sites, and remain popular through the Late Byzantine period. Although 'frying pans' are also found in the Early Byzantine period, their increasing numbers may imply that cooking practices had changed, perhaps with more fried or parched food consumed. The disuse of chafing dishes and fruit stands might imply that meals were structured differently as part of this change in eating habits.

Consequently, ceramics can suggest how food may have been prepared and consumed, and how this might have changed over time. Combined with artistic (and the few relevant written) sources, ceramic evidence implies that in each of the major periods of Byzantine history food and drink was prepared, served and eaten in different ways. It will in future be possible to use analysis of the residues found within vessels and the sealed contents of amphorae to tell us even more of Byzantine food and eating habits, but insufficient data on this exists currently to enable any general observations based on such evidence.

Pottery can also tell us much more about the everyday life of the Byzantine population. One surprising aspect that it illuminates is changing dress and hairstyle fashions. The stamps and painted designs on Early Byzantine pottery produced in North Africa, Egypt and Syria depict people wearing exactly the same sort of dress and hairstyles as shown in Late Roman and Early Byzantine mosaics and wall paintings, for example in the sixth century at San Vitale in Ravenna.

Most men and all women wear long flowing garments, sometimes with ornamental patches and with belts around the waist. Some men wear long trousers. Men have short or medium-length hair (by which I mean hair above the shoulder); women wear mostly medium-length hair. Most men are clean-shaven. Even details of jewellery are sometimes shown on these stamped designs, again reflecting what we know from surviving examples of early Byzantine jewellery and from other, more formal, artistic sources.

Although not adding greatly to our knowledge of Early Byzantine dress and hairstyles, these depictions support the view that other art indicates the realities of Early Byzantine appearance. It seems that people really did look like this, at least in the areas where these ceramics were produced.

Relatively few depictions of human figures are found on Middle Byzantine pottery compared to Early Byzantine vessels. Although saints are shown on some Polychrome Ware tiles, these are the conventionalized images of Middle Byzantine church art. They are highly stylized and governed by formal rules of representation. However, Polychrome Ware occasionally depicts people in ways that may represent the realities of contemporary appearance. For example, a man with a beard and medium-length hair wearing a knee-length tunic is shown on one vessel, another shows a bearded man with short hair in a similar tunic wearing a turban.

Figural depiction becomes common again in the latter part of the Middle Byzantine period. Fine Sgraffito Ware vessels show men with mid-length or long hair and wearing long tunics. This may suggest that men wore their hair longer during the Middle Byzantine period than had been common before *c*.700, and perhaps that beards were more commonly worn, again supporting depictions in other media. But it seems from this evidence that tunics reaching at least to just above the knees, with or without trousers, remained standard male attire until the twelfth century.

The first strong evidence of different clothing fashions comes from pottery only after *c*.1200. On Late Byzantine Coloured Sgraffito Ware male figures wear short 'kilts', not tunics or trousers. Male hairstyles appear to have remained long: on one Champleve Ware plate from Corinth, depicting a 'courting couple', the man has longer hair than the woman. A warrior depicted on an Incised Sgraffito Ware bowl in the Louvre seems to have a pointed helmet, a rectangular shield, spear, and knee-length mail coat.[3]

This may suggest that men wore their hair increasingly long during the Middle and Late Byzantine period and that tunics and trousers were replaced by 'kilts'. The appearance of figures in 'Western' medieval dress on thirteenth-century and later vessels may suggest that Western fashions were also adopted after that time. Women appear veiled for the first time and often they wear clothes that would not be out of place in a contemporary Western medieval context. If these are depictions of everyday reality, and not intended for Westerners, it seems that Late Byzantine clothing had been affected by 'Westernization', although some distinctive fashions, notably the turbans worn by some men, persisted.

Possibly even more surprising than its contribution to the history of Byzantine fashion is the contribution that ceramics offer to the study of Middle and Late Byzantine popular literature, music and dance. Scenes on Incised Sgraffito Ware and Measles Ware vessels appear to show Digenes Akritas, the fictional Byzantine hero of the eastern Anatolian borderland, sometimes in specific adventures recognizable from the surviving versions of his story. These vessels had a wide distribution in Greece and the Crimea, but seem less common in Anatolia, although that is where the story is set.[4]

46 Late Byzantine Incised Sgraffito Ware sherd depicting a musician playing a stringed instrument, in the Victoria and Albert Museum

Depictions on Late Byzantine pottery also include men playing an instrument like a lute and female dancers in long skirts holding something like castanets. The rarity of Late Byzantine depictions of music-making and dancing, outside church contexts, renders these of considerable potential interest to students of the history of music and dance, as well as for Late Byzantine society. Even Byzantine humour is occasionally represented. For example, a chafing dish has models of monkeys holding their noses, presumably from the smell of the food![5]

Pottery also provides information about Byzantine burial practices. It is often said by scholars debating western European burial practices that Christians never put objects in the grave. Not only is this, in fact, untrue in western Europe during the first millennium AD, but Byzantine evidence shows it to be false in the Orthodox Christian world.[6]

The Byzantines often placed pottery vessels (and other objects) in graves, even when those graves were within consecrated ground or inside churches. This was especially true of drinking vessels (cups and jugs), although pottery bowls and plates were also deposited in graves. For example, pottery cups were placed in Late Byzantine graves both at the church of St Demetrios and at the Hippodrome at Thessaloniki.[7]

In fact, the use of pottery vessels as grave-goods was a very long-lived practice in the Byzantine world. It is first attested in the Early Byzantine period, where it was widespread in the eastern Mediterranean. Examples include the church of St Dionysios the Areopagite at Athens (where Early Byzantine unglazed jugs were put in graves) and Byzantine Palestine, where for example the grave of a soldier by the Red Sea was furnished with an ARSW plate.[8]

The use of pottery vessels in graves also occurred throughout the Middle and Late Byzantine Empire. For example, at Saraçhane, Late Byzantine graves contained pottery vessels. It may have been especially common in Post-Byzantine Cyprus. Nonetheless, the use of grave-goods seems always to have been a minority rite and the majority of burials contain no artefacts at all. Moreover, not only Byzantine pottery was used in this way, Islamic vessels have been reported from inside thirteenth- and fourteenth-century Byzantine tombs at St John's church in Ephesus.[9]

Although published data are insufficient to allow certainty, there seems some regularity in the way that pottery was used in funerary customs. For example, both at Athens and in the Agora at Corinth, unglazed jugs accompanied burials which otherwise contained no pottery and only a few other gravegoods, including buckles perhaps indicating clothed burial. So we may be looking at a burial rite, rather than an individualistic custom of particular families or people.

The reason for this practice is unknown. However, it may relate to the beliefs — popular in modern rural Greek Orthodox folk-religion — that the soul must make a journey to Heaven, and that souls still need to eat and drink physical food. Food and drink may have been provided to sustain the soul on this journey, and placed in the grave in pottery vessels.[10]

Whatever the reason, the inclusion of pottery in the grave contrasts with the Western medieval (and modern) Christian norm of burial without any gravegoods. The study of pottery can, therefore, tell us about Byzantine burial practices and their contrasts with medieval Western customs. It can also contribute to broader archaeological debates about interpreting burial data.

Consequently, we can see that pottery is a valuable source for reconstructing aspects of everyday life (and burial practice) in the Byzantine Empire. Ceramics may also help us to understand aspects of Byzantine art, such as the nature of art and relationship between art and design in different media.

Fine-ware as fine art

Byzantine fine-wares are closely related to broader artistic trends. Designs known from sculpture, textiles and other media are repeated almost unchanged on fine-ware pottery. This is true of the relationship between these media, so that textiles, frescos, sculpture and enamels all share a common artistic culture, which is also shared by fine-ware pottery.

In the Early Byzantine period and, especially, in the Middle Byzantine period, pottery was often decorated with designs identical to those found in other media. These designs have, in the past, been used as a means of dating Byzantine pottery, but their significance may be much greater than this. As independent forms of dating for pottery and these other media exist, it is possible to explore the connections between them in new ways and in particular to recognize the social range of what might otherwise appear to be 'high art'.

Early Byzantine pottery is a particularly rich source for reconstructing pre-Iconoclast popular art, including religious art. Even the growth of Christianity to become the religion of the majority of the Byzantine population can be traced to some extent through the fourth- and fifth-century religious art of red-slip and

47 Examples of crosses and other religious symbols found on Early Byzantine red-slip wares. After Hayes

local fine-wares, as specifically Christian designs were increasingly used.[11]

Many of the Early Byzantine depictions of saints on red-slipped wares and pilgrim flasks also attest to naturalism in the art of Early Byzantine pottery. This naturalism is found in a more accomplished form in contemporary non-ceramic art, such as the sixth-century icons from St Catherine's monastery, Sinai. However, pottery vessels demonstrate the generality of naturalistic representation in relatively 'low-status' contexts, from which we have few other examples of contemporary art.[12]

Likewise, the changing form of Christian symbolism is very well documented by depictions on pottery. Different forms of Chi Rho symbols and of the cross that were introduced at different times may be dated on the evidence of fine-ware forms. These depictions may assist the art historian tracing the development of Christian symbolism in the Byzantine East, just as the dated series of crosses from the Catacombs at Rome assist those undertaking the same exercise in the West. Obviously, such evidence has to be set alongside other artistic representations, but again pottery may be a useful source of well-dated material for the reconstruction of pre-Iconoclast Byzantine religious art.[13]

The decline in religious depictions on eighth- and ninth-century Byzantine pottery could be related to the Iconoclast movement. With the exception of a few cross-symbols (which were acceptable even in Iconoclast art), no certainly religious depictions on Middle Byzantine ceramics need to date before the end of state-sponsored Iconoclasm. This stands in such a contrast to Early Byzantine fine-wares that it is possible that the religious environment of the seventh to ninth centuries in some respect affected the

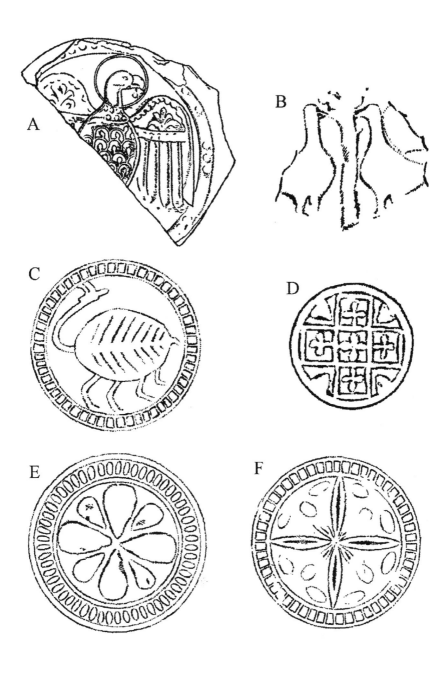

48 *Designs found on Middle Byzantine Impressed Ware. All from Corinth except A,*
which may be from Istanbul. After Talbot Rice and Morgan

decline in images of saints and other religious figures on pottery, although this is necessarily uncertain.

Whether or not the decline in religious depictions on Byzantine pottery in the eighth and ninth century is related to Iconoclasm, designs found on Middle Byzantine pottery after the ninth century are strongly reminiscent of other contemporary art. For example, one might compare the decoration of Polychrome Ware and the wall paintings of the Cappadocian rock-cut buildings (the so-called 'cave monasteries') of Middle Byzantine date.[14]

Impressed Ware stamps include religious depictions. For example, one sherd shows a mounted warrior saint and another shows an enigmatic image (published here for the first time), probably of an apsed and domed Byzantine church. This may be the only depiction of a Middle Byzantine building on pottery, although models of churches were made in Middle Byzantine whitewares, probably forming parts of chafing dishes. Polychrome Ware tiles also carry an elaborate range of religious images. Again, this was probably not until after the restoration of icons to Orthodox worship.[15]

The similarity between the decoration of Middle Byzantine fine-ware and other forms of art is well illustrated by the designs found cut into the centres of eleventh- and twelfth-century Fine Sgraffito Ware plates. For example, the scenes of a lion devouring a stag as its prey, eagles with outspread wings, and sitting hares are shared with sculpture and textiles, as are the mythological animals depicted, such as griffins.[16]

On Fine Sgraffito Ware such scenes are drawn in a very similar style and composition from one vessel to the next, although layout on the vessel varies. However, even variation in layout is not random and this enables distinctive decorational style to be recognized.

On this basis, Morgan divided the designs found on Byzantine sgraffito products into 'Medallion', 'Intermediate' and 'Free' styles. The 'Medallion Style' has a central basal interior medallion, usually surrounded by two concentric bands of decoration. The 'Intermediate Style' has no central medallion but has figural subjects in the centre of the interior, usually surrounded by single incised decorative band. The 'Free Style' has no centering of the figural design nor surrounding band and a much more 'spreading' design occupies the whole of the interior surface. One can also recognize an 'Aniconic Style', which has no figural subject but only geometric or foliate decoration, spread across the interior.[17]

It seems possible that these styles represent phases of manufacture, with the earliest the 'Medallion Style', followed by the 'Intermediate Style', then the 'Free Style', and finally the 'Aniconic Style'. The first two were executed in Fine Sgraffito Ware (the 'Medallion Style' in particular is well coin-dated in excavated deposits at Corinth), but the 'Free' and 'Aniconic' styles are associated with Coloured Sgraffito Ware of thirteenth-century or later date. In fact, the latter lasted well beyond the Byzantine period in Greek folk pottery in association with the continued production of Coloured Sgraffito Ware.

Distinctive regional preferences in decorative subject can be found too. At present, these are usually insufficiently studied to permit different regional styles

49 Examples of designs found on Polychrome Ware tiles. After Talbot Rice

to be compared across the Empire or the basis of these regional tastes to be established. For example, there seem to be differences in the frequency with which mythological animals are depicted: centaurs seem more common in Greece, but griffons more common in Anatolia. One place where a regional style seems well attested is at Thessaloniki, where Late Byzantine fine-wares show a remarkable preference for bird designs, 'hatched circle', cross or star motifs. These designs enable one to recognize a Late Byzantine Thessalonikan product easily and suggest a degree of shared local identity.[18]

The designs in the centres of Fine Sgraffito Ware plates of the 'Medallion' and 'Intermediate' styles in particular seem so standardized that it is possible that the use of pattern-books explains this. The evidence for the production of extremely similar Fine Sgraffito Ware vessels in several centres seems to exclude the main alternative possibility of a single producer or even regional tradition accounting for these similarities in design.

The possibility that pattern books lie behind these similarities brings us back to the relationship with art in other media. The use of pattern-books may also explain the shared designs found on Fine Sgraffito Ware and twelfth-century Byzantine metalwork, textiles and sculpture. This would suggest that the same pattern-books were in use for art in different media.

If designs were shared between pottery and other works of art, it may be legitimate to combine evidence from all of these media in discussions of Byzantine art history. For example, symbolism, such as that of animals hunting and birds of prey (possibly, as Eunice Dauterman Maguire has argued, evoking images of energy and might), frequently appears as part of sgraffito ware pottery decoration. Understanding the meaning of designs found on pottery may, therefore, help us to understand what such images mean across the range of Byzantine art, although this might of course have varied depending upon context and date. Perhaps more importantly, the sharing of designs, and possibly pattern-books, between potters and other artists suggests that pottery decoration was seen by Byzantines in this period as art, not simply a distinct 'crafts tradition' separate from other spheres of artistic activity.[19]

That elements of 'Islamic art' were employed by potters to decorate objects for Byzantine homes may imply that Byzantine observers did not perceive all designs as symbolic. The use of pseudo-Kufic lettering on fine-ware suggests that this was not seen as necessarily carrying religious messages contrary to Byzantine beliefs, or having unacceptable political associations. From this it seems that design could be appreciated by potters and by 'consumers' simply as decoration, suggesting a more 'neutral' or 'secular' manner of thought than many modern scholars have been inclined to attribute to Byzantine observers.

The study of Byzantine pottery can, therefore, make a unique contribution to the study of art. Pottery also forms a surprisingly useful source for discussing the changing identity of the Byzantine Empire.

Pottery and the identity of Byzantium

A key question in Byzantine Studies has long been to what extent the Byzantine Empire remained a 'Roman' or even 'Classical' society after the seventh century. We have already seen that fine-ware pottery underwent major changes in the seventh century, as did many other aspects of the Byzantine world. In particular, the shift from red-slipped wares to glazed whitewares can be seen in terms of a fashion change occurring at this time. However, even fashion change has to have an explanation. In this case, the explanation may lie in the cultural associations of the red-slipped wares and glazed whitewares.

The popularity of Early Byzantine red-slipped wares may be partly explained by an aesthetic taste for red-coloured fine-ware in the Roman Empire. No equivalent high-quality red-coloured pottery was manufactured outside the Mediterranean, although grey- and orange-coloured imitations were produced in Gaul and Spain in local fabrics.[20]

It is also possible that the 'red' colour of these fine-wares held specifically 'Roman' associations for contemporaries, although it is unclear what precisely these associations were. Possibly, the 'imperial purple' of the Empire was evoked by what we see as 'red' slip, or maybe it recalled the red colour of Roman military cloaks. Perhaps red-slipped pottery itself 'looked Roman' — after all, red-slipped wares had been popular in the Empire for centuries.

Whatever the basis of this symbolism, an association with the Roman world could have rendered red-slipped pottery desirable to those people and communities wishing to evoke *Romanitas* ('Roman-ness') in the fifth and sixth centuries. This may be the attraction that led to these wares being very widely traded beyond imperial frontiers to the West, to communities where *Romanitas* remained a source of political or religious legitimation and cultural identity for at least some of the population.

Red-slipped pottery was not produced in Constantinople. It was manufactured in the provinces and marketed on a regional level. By contrast, the glazed whitewares were associated with the political centre of the Empire and were initially probably exported directly from the centre to the remaining provinces.

This contrast may suggest that Early Byzantine red-slipped fine-ware and Middle Byzantine whitewares held different political or cultural associations. In particular, using whitewares may have symbolized a greater attachment to the capital, at a time when this offered both a sense of security and 'Roman' identity challenged by the circumstances of the seventh and eighth centuries. In the face of the expansion of the Arab political control, communities throughout the Byzantine Empire may have asserted their 'Roman' and 'Christian' identity, and might have used material culture, including pottery, in order to achieve this.[21]

Alternatively, perhaps, the white colour was perceived to represent purity or holiness, as in Byzantine art in general. Whiteness might have expressed a more explicitly 'Christian' than 'imperial' identity, although these identities may not have been divisible in many seventh- and eighth-century Byzantine minds.

The distribution of the whitewares may support this interpretation. During the fifth and sixth centuries red-slipped wares were used in all parts of what had been the Roman Empire in 400. They are even found in Britain, but only on sites occupied by descendents of the former Roman provincials. By contrast, Middle Byzantine whitewares, including both Polychrome Ware and CWW, are very seldom found outside the Empire, even in Italy. The only exceptions were regions with very strong religious and political links with the Empire, especially Bulgaria and Russia.

This suggests that the distribution of both classes of pottery was to some extent either politically or culturally constrained, but not in the same way. If using red-slipped wares in the fifth and sixth centuries meant 'being Roman', perhaps using Byzantine whitewares in the eighth to tenth centuries meant 'being Byzantine' (as we would term it) or 'being Orthodox'.

This interpretation is supported if we look again at the evidence provided by Impressed Ware. The exact reason why Impressed Ware was stamped remains unclear. John Hayes has suggested that, because some of the stamps are very indistinct, they served as maker's-marks, while David Talbot Rice believed they were part of the vessels' decoration. As Judith Herrin has noted, some Impressed Ware pottery-stamps resemble those found in other Byzantine contexts, such as bread-stamps.[22]

It may well be doubted whether lack of clarity is a distinguishing characteristic of maker's-marks. One might expect producers to prefer maker's-marks to be

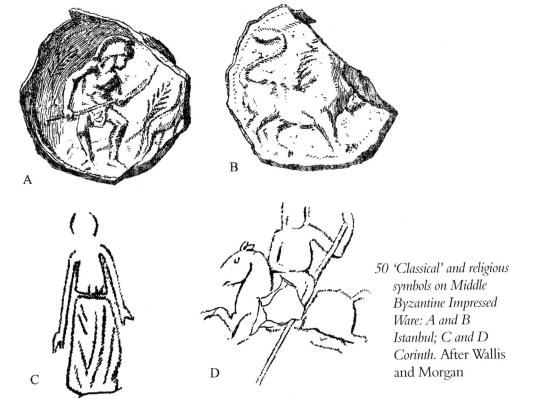

50 'Classical' and religious symbols on Middle Byzantine Impressed Ware: A and B Istanbul; C and D Corinth. After Wallis and Morgan

easily seen. Moreover, on many vessels the stamps are clear enough to be seen by the users. It may well be that the lack of clarity in some cases is nothing more than the result of either poor technical execution or the use of worn-out dies for stamping the vessels. Consequently, while they could also have had a function as maker's-marks, it may be more likely that the stamps were meant as part of the vessels' decoration.

A striking aspect of these designs is their Classicism. The rendition of subjects such as eagles and lions, although popular in the Roman period, might be explained away as simply motifs displaying an interest in the drama of wild predatory animals. Nevertheless, the use of a haloed eagle on Impressed Ware bowls suggests an Imperial association, and much more self-consciously Classical subjects were also selected for display on other pieces of Impressed Ware.

Some Impressed Ware sherds show figures dressed in Classical costume, reminiscent of early Roman Imperial art. Such figures occur elsewhere in Middle Byzantine art and are usually interpreted as deliberately antiquarian, suitable for learned or aristocratic audiences familiar with Roman history and the continuing assertion of the Empire's Roman identity.

However, Classical designs placed on pottery were known both to the potters who manufactured these vessels and seen by a broad range of the Middle Byzantine population. Pottery decoration may, in this respect, demonstrate that self-conscious Classicism — like an interest in Islamic art — was not the preserve of a small elite. If these depictions were recognizably 'Classical' to people using the pottery, then this suggests that the Middle Byzantine population in general may have been keener to assert its 'Roman' heritage than we might assume on the basis of other evidence.

This does not, of course, mean that either the artists decorating Impressed Ware or their customers had much accurate understanding of the Roman past. But it may imply that the Byzantine population recognized what we would see as 'Classical art' as symbolic of that Roman past. This is unsurprising, given that this population was in many cases living literally amid the ruins of Classical antiquity. But it is still remarkable that anyone thought it worthwhile to copy this art on pottery stamps.

The evocation of the Classical past may also explain mythological designs on Late Byzantine ceramics. These include Perseus, centaurs, and Medusa — figures from Classical myth and presumably either part of currently circulating story or another facet of this antiquarian tendency.[23]

It is even possible that Early Byzantine ceramic art was imitated, or preserved, in Middle Byzantine fine-ware decoration. Crosses stamped on Middle Byzantine Impressed Ware include examples very similar to those on Early Byzantine fine-wares, impressed onto the centre of the pot with a stamp in the same way as their possible Early Byzantine models. This could, of course, have happened by chance, but it could be evidence of a continuing or revived Early Byzantine practice.

Such self-consciously 'antiquarian' designs found on Middle Byzantine fine-wares have to be set alongside the preservation of the Early Byzantine coarse-ware ceramic repertoire into the Middle Byzantine period. Formal change did occur, but this was no more than one sees in Roman ceramics during an equivalent part of the first to fourth centuries. The range of coarse-ware vessels and their overall appearance varied little from the fifth to twelfth centuries.

The evidence from amphorae supports this pattern of general continuity. Trivial details of formal change are perhaps more noticeable to a modern ceramic typologist than a Byzantine amphora-user. If anything, 'high handled' amphorae characteristic of the Middle Byzantine period bear more, not less, resemblance to earlier Roman amphora forms than Early Byzantine amphorae. 'High handled' forms were common before the fifth century but passed out of fashion, before their revival in the Middle Byzantine period.[24]

In ceramic terms — that is, in terms of a category of objects found in almost every Byzantine home — a great amount of the Roman past *was* preserved in Middle Byzantine everyday life. In terms of coarse-ware use, little changed in Byzantine material culture between the fifth and twelfth centuries. So perhaps it should not surprise us that there was still a 'Roman' identity left to evoke among the majority of the population. The Middle Byzantine period appears from this material more 'Roman', and possibly less 'medieval', than we might suppose on other grounds.[25]

Ceramics may, then, more fully reflect the culture and identity of the bulk of the Byzantine population than sources such as sculpture, fine metalwork and frescos, let alone surviving texts. Yet it would be a mistake to suppose that all Byzantine pottery necessarily betokens a 'lower-status art form': the opposite may be true in relation to Polychrome Ware tiles. The distinctive designs of early Polychrome Ware have prompted much comment as to their source and character, but an overlooked aspect of their significance is their potential as a source for imperial diplomacy and patronage.

Polychrome Ware tiles and imperial patronage

There is a strong connection between Polychrome Ware tiles and the Imperial Court at Constantinople. At least two written references perhaps refer to the use of decorative tiles in the Great Palace: when the Emperor Basil I refurbished the palace in the ninth century he added at least one tiled walkway, while a tile bearing the depiction of Christ seems to have been later visible in the chapel at the Chrysotriklinos. Archaeology confirms the use of Polychrome Ware tiles within the palace. Many such tiles were found during Turkish excavations at the site in the 1980s, associated with a structure with an opus sectile floor containing a mosaic panel, suggesting that it was a prestigious building. This may suggest that Polychrome Ware tiles were visible in a number of parts of the palace during the ninth century and later.[26]

It has already been suggested that Polychrome Ware was manufactured in the Palace itself, and the possibility that Polychrome Ware tiles were made there must also be considered. In this context, it may be interesting to compare the tiles with the frescos of a building excavated in 1998 by the eminent Turkish archaeologist Dr Aplay Pasinli on a site between Hagia Sophia and the mosque of Sultan Ahmet in Istanbul. The excavated evidence includes a fresco with a series of polychrome geometric and floral designs on a very pale background, adorning the walls of a vaulted room. The decoration closely resembles that found on some Polychrome Ware tiles and pottery, and could suggest that this reflected broader decorative schemes in imperial buildings at the heart of the Byzantine capital.[27]

Whether or not the latter is a meaningful link, more light is thrown on the tiles by their known distribution in Constantinople. They have been found at only two categories of building: churches with imperial connections or structures within (or very closely related to) the Great Palace.

Other than these, the Byzantine-produced Polychrome Ware tiles have seldom been found on sites that were inside the Empire. One group is from a church at Usbubu, Duzce (Prusias ad Hypium) in what was Byzantine Bithynia. Another has a confused provenance but could be from the Asiatic side of the Bosphorus. Polychrome Ware tiles are also visible on a photograph of the destroyed mosaics at the Byzantine church of the Dormition at Iznik (Nicaea).[28]

The imperial contacts of the first pair of sites, if any, are unknown. However, the provincial location of these two outlying find-spots may suggest that external patronage or special circumstances led to these buildings. No other structures in their general area were provided with these tiles.

It may be relevant that Prusias ad Hypium was near Nicomedia, from which the tiles that decorated the church of the 'Palace of Botaneites' in Constantinople are said to have come. 'Glazed tiles of Nicomedia' were mentioned when the former Byzantine palace passed into Genoese ownership in the thirteenth century, but whether or not the writer who provided this description was well-informed about the origin of these tiles, or even of Byzantine tiles in general, is unclear. It is not even certain, although likely, that they were what we would call Polychrome Ware tiles.

The Middle Byzantine Polychrome Ware tiles at Nicaea might be explained either because this city was a centre of patronage (it held a Byzantine court after the fall of Constantinople in 1204) or by proximity to one of the manufacturing centres. The Middle Byzantine importance of the church of the Dormition at Nicaea could easily have attracted an imperial gift of tiles.

Polychrome Ware tiles may, therefore, have a strong association with imperial construction projects. A specific connection with the Court is further supported if we look at the use of Polychrome Ware tiles and imitations of these outside the Empire. Beyond the Byzantine frontier, Polychrome Ware tiles have been found at Preslav and elsewhere in Bulgaria. But evidence for their manufacture there, in no way contradicts an imperial association. The Bulgarian court attempted to emulate Byzantine courtly life and the manufacture of Polychrome Ware tiles may mimic the courtly production of these prestigious ceramics at Constantinople. Strange as it might appear to a modern observer, it may have seemed more, not less, like the Great Palace of the Byzantine emperors in Constantinople, to have potters making tiles in the Bulgarian court.[29]

This association would also explain the Byzantine imperial gift of Polychrome Ware tiles to the Emir for the mosque at Cordoba in Spain. The Emir wrote specifically to the Byzantine Emperor to request some of these tiles. If the tiles were available on the 'open market' obviously such a request would have been unnecessary and this incident may, therefore, imply that the only way to obtain such tiles was directly from the Imperial Court.[30]

If the Byzantine Court controlled the distribution of the tiles, their mere presence might then have represented an imperial connection and their decoration might — as we have seen — have evoked that of the Great Palace. As such, Polychrome Ware tiles can be seen as objects of exceptional status and diplomatic importance. Their existence at any site may suggest a courtly connection, probably direct imperial patronage of the building if within the Empire or diplomatic contacts with the Court if outside.

This new interpretation of Polychrome Ware tiles need not necessarily preclude the later more widespread manufacture of Polychrome Ware vessels, as these may not have always carried the same associations. But this is no reason to doubt that the tiles, at least, held special importance. This may well be why they remain somewhat rare finds, especially outside Constantinople.

It was not just Polychrome Ware tiles that could become diplomatic gifts. Elaborate Incised Ware may also have been produced for diplomatic purposes. In particular, the elaborately decorated bowl called today the 'Constantine Bowl', now in The British Museum, may be an example of an Elaborate Incised Ware bowl commissioned as a diplomatic gift.[31]

Conclusion

Thus, pottery provides us with a valuable source for many aspects of Byzantine life relatively unevidenced by texts and other art forms. It is, then, an error to ignore the potential of this source for the study of Byzantine culture. Finally, it is important to explore when and how this ceramic tradition came to an end.

6 Conclusion: the end of the Byzantine Empire and beyond

Although Byzantine pottery, as defined here, ends in the fifteenth century, production seems to have continued to form the basis for Balkan, Cypriot, Greek and Turkish 'folk pottery'. Direct evidence for continuing production has been found in several areas. At Khania on Crete a workshop continuously manufactured pottery from the fifteenth century at latest until the late Ottoman period. On Cyprus, Byzantine pottery-making traditions continued under both Western and Ottoman rule, producing a distinctive series of vessels that look 'Byzantine' at first sight. 'Random Painted Wares' of ultimately Byzantine origin were produced in fifteenth- and sixteenth-century Greece and, as already noted, the 'Aniconic' style of Coloured Sgraffito Ware also continued throughout the fifteenth and sixteenth centuries, in some areas into the nineteenth century.[1]

In the Balkans too, Late Byzantine pottery-types such as Coloured Sgraffito Ware, Slip-Painted Ware and Incised Sgraffito Ware continued in production beyond the end of Byzantine rule and throughout the Ottoman period. The characteristic Late Byzantine ceramics manufactured in Thessaloniki, with their distinctive glaze and bird designs, were still produced into the Ottoman period and the glazed redwares of Constantinople continued in production after the Ottoman conquest.[2]

Mark Whittow has drawn attention to a class of everted rimmed water jars with pinched banding, manufactured in a light red micaceous fabric with white inclusions, produced into the twentieth century by village potters in western Anatolia. Such jars resemble closely those found in eighth- to eleventh-century layers at Pammukale (Hieropolis). These might, then, represent local pottery produced continuously through, and beyond, the later part of the Byzantine period.[3]

Demonstrating actual continuity of production at kiln sites is nonetheless very hard. On mainland Greece, the sites at Veria and Trikala, in addition to the city of Thessaloniki itself, have all shown direct evidence for Post-Byzantine pottery production. In the latter case, this was apparently right in the centre of the Ottoman city, near the famous Rotunda. But none of these sites definitely had Byzantine period kilns in the same area.[4]

The problem of demonstrating continuity from Byzantine to Ottoman production even at a well-studied site is illustrated at Didymoteichon. This was a major centre of pottery manufacture from the seventeenth century onward, and over 200 separate producers operated in the vicinity in the seventeenth century according to the Turkish writer Evliya Celebi.[5]

What might be evidence of Late Byzantine production has been found at the site, but this is ambiguous. However, in the early Post-Byzantine period it was producing a wide range of pottery. This included both 'Byzantine' and 'Ottoman' vessels, such as Coloured Sgraffito Ware, coarse-wares of both Late Byzantine and Ottoman appearance, green glazed vessels in pink-buff fabric with white slip, Slip-Painted Ware, relief-decorated jugs with dotted roundels, 'Ottoman' marbled ware, and trefoil-mouthed jugs. But it remains unclear if production started during the Byzantine period or shortly after.

One surprising aspect of Post-Byzantine pottery production was the manufacture of imitations of Italian Proto-Maiolica in fifteenth- and sixteenth-century Post-Byzantine contexts. This shows a continuing taste for Italian fine-wares on the part of Post-Byzantine communities, attested also by the continuing importation of such pottery.

The hardest problem in relating Byzantine to Ottoman pottery is the possible link between Middle Byzantine Polychrome Ware and the famous Ottoman Iznik ceramics. The latter are usually considered among the finest Ottoman pottery and tile. It seems a coincidence that the leading focus of Ottoman polychrome whiteware vessel and tile production was an area in which Byzantine Polychrome Ware manufacture may have also been located.

Byzantine whiteware wasters have been recognised by Veronique François at Iznik. Nevertheless, establishing a link bridging centuries of apparent discontinuity from the probable end of Byzantine whiteware production to the start of Ottoman Iznik pottery is still extremely difficult. Similarly, there are differences between the technology of Byzantine whitewares and of Ottoman Iznik pottery (especially in the preparation of the clay) that might render the superficial similarities illusory.

One possibility is that the localized production of whitewares survived at Iznik up to the end of the Byzantine period and was modified by later technological and artistic change. It is, therefore, possible that Iznik pottery represents the continuation of whiteware production at Nicaea extending back into the Middle Byzantine period, but this is a topic in need of further research. Here, as elsewhere in the former Byzantine Empire, it is at present unclear how close a relationship existed between the Byzantine and Ottoman ceramic traditions.[6]

Catalogue of pottery types

Introduction

This catalogue aims to assist the identification of the main classes of Byzantine glazed or decorated pottery which may be of most help in dating or interpreting assemblages in excavations, museums or surface-surveys. Careful use will enable reliable identifications and approximate dates to be assigned to pottery assemblages, prior to specialist study. Specialist examination will, of course, provide much more detailed information, especially in relation to Early Byzantine fine-wares.

Methods used in compiling the catalogue

For each class I have given a date-range, generalized distribution and possible source. These sections have been compiled on the following basis. Dating is entirely based on coin-dated stratigraphically excavated deposits and, as a consequence of their availability at present, chronologies for the period before *c*.700 are much more accurate than for later centuries. For the Early Byzantine period many well-excavated and coin-dated stratified pottery sequences are known. Particularly important are those in Istanbul, Carthage, Rome and Athens.

These provide extremely good dating for the commonest Early Byzantine fine-wares, such as ARSW and PRSW. Nevertheless, even in the fifth and sixth centuries some chronological reordering may still occur as more coin-dated deposits are excavated and some classes are far better dated than others.

Middle Byzantine coin-dated stratified assemblages are far fewer than those of the earlier period. Consequently, dating after *c*.700 has to be broader and less certain. The excavated assemblages from Athens, Sparta, Pergamon and most of all Istanbul and Corinth, are the mainstays of the ceramic chronology for this period. This generally enables broad dates to be assigned to specific wares, but these lack the chronological precision of Early Byzantine fine-ware.

Ceramics incorporated in architecture (such as the vessels, known as *bacini*, incorporated into Italian churches) may provide an additional source of dating evidence. However, this depends upon detailed 'structural criticism' of the buildings involved. This is not possible for plastered, or otherwise obscured, structures and there are obvious problems of reuse and curation to complicate this issue. Most examples in Italy and Greece occur late in the Byzantine pottery sequence and relate only to the Late Byzantine phase of production. They are of more limited help in establishing dates for most of the material encompassed in this book than might be imagined.

Laboratory-based dating methods have not yet been applied to Byzantine pottery as a whole, nor are these yet so refined as to always distinguish, for example, eleventh-century pottery from that of the twelfth century. So laboratory science is of little use in providing Middle and Late Byzantine pottery with a more secure chronology at present, other than in the recognition of fakes.

Consequently, dating of most of the pottery described here is necessarily expressed in broad terms. Middle and Late Byzantine pottery may yet be found which pre-date or post-date known examples by decades, given the very limited degree to which this material has been systematically identified and examined in stratified sequences.

This approximate dating is expressed here by centuries, shown in Roman numerals. This provides a realistic assessment of the low level of chronological precision currently available for Middle and Late Byzantine pottery. For example, VII = seventh century. The symbol < is used to indicate 'and earlier' and > for 'and later'.

Most Early Byzantine fine-wares are capable of very much closer dating but, for consistency, similar broad date-ranges are given here for these. In such cases, a star indicates where the reader should consult sources (cited in the chapter notes) providing more detailed chronologies.

The source of each class — the place or places in which that class was produced — has been established on one or more of three grounds: the presence of kilns, the presence of wasters, and laboratory techniques offering possible geological source areas for the clay used. Again, there is a difference between earlier wares, which are mostly provenanced by kilns, wasters and geological evidence, and Middle and Late Byzantine wares, which are often less certainly provenanced.

Sources are shown in relation to modern countries (such as Greece or Bulgaria) and well-known geographical regions (such as Anatolia, the Balkans or the Aegean islands) or in relation to the Byzantine capital itself. In the latter case, 'Constantinople region' indicates not the Byzantine walled city alone, but its surrounding European and Asian hinterland. 'Cyprus' refers to the whole island in its geographical sense and 'Palestine' to the former Byzantine province, including what is today Israel but extending beyond its present borders. 'Southern Greece' refers to the Peloponnese. 'North Africa' is used to designate those areas of Africa north of the Sahara formerly under Roman rule, except for the region encompassed by modern Egypt, which is designated under the name of the modern country. Obviously, it would be possible to use other divisions, but these designations should suffice to indicate both source areas and distributions. Source areas are listed alphabetically, except for the Byzantine capital which is placed first where relevant, unless this would obscure the particular association of a class with a geographical area.

Distribution is also expressed here in general terms, rather than by reference to specific sites, and employs the same geographical terminology. Generalized distributions are used here because publication of this pottery has been (and is) so uneven and differential that one cannot always establish the presence or absence of a class of pottery from any site or area. Quantification, while this will help clarify distributions in future, is not currently possible at most relevant sites dating from after *c*.700. Finally, there is the crucial matter of how the individual wares are defined. A central problem of Byzantine pottery studies is the varying terminology used in publications. This is resolved here by modifying conventional terminology to make it more precise. Hopefully, the clarification of definitions in this catalogue will assist greater consistency in the description of Byzantine pottery in the future.

As a result of this method of compiling the catalogue, specialists will find a degree of variation between the dating assigned to particular classes here and conventional dates for these. For example, the detailed chronologies frequently assigned to Byzantine sgraffito wares seem, on these grounds, unjustified and are not employed in this book.

African Red Slip Ware (=ARSW)

A slightly granular, orange to (often) brick-red micaceous fabric, often the latter, sometimes slightly pinkish. Inclusions are limestone and other white, brown or even black particles. The overall slip is almost the same colour as the body, but slightly darker.

The exterior and interior surfaces are very smooth and perhaps were originally polished. Stamped decoration occurs, alongside incision and relief modeling. Often the stamps in the interior base are surrounded by grooves, perhaps in imitation of metalwork.

Exceptionally well-dated form and motif typologies exist for this class. Motifs include religious, human, animal, floral, and geometric designs.

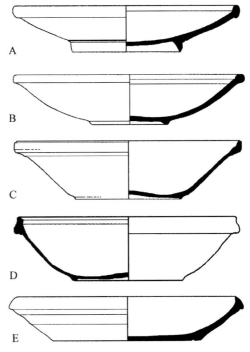

Date:	<V-VII★
Source:	North Africa, especially the Carthage area
Distribution:	Found in the whole of what was, in *c*.400, the Roman Empire

Phocaean Red Slip Ware

A very standardized ware with a slightly micaceous fabric. The fabric ranges in colour from red-brown to

51 Examples of forms of African, Phocaean and Cypriot Red Slip Wares: A and B ARSW; C and D PRSW; E CRSW. After Hayes

purplish-red but is lighter than the overall slip, which may be either matt or glossy. It is both harder than African Red Slip Ware (ARSW) and unlike ARSW it often has rouletted decoration.

A range of well-dated forms and motifs occur but bowls were the commonest product. Stamped decoration encompassing human, religious, mythological, floral, animal, and geometric motifs is found.

Date: <V-VII★
Source: Phocaea in western Anatolia
Distribution: Found in the whole of what was, in *c*.400, the Roman Empire

Cypriot Red Slip Ware (=CRSW)

A yellow-orange, red or purple coloured fabric with limestone inclusions. The overall slip is similar in colour to the body, but darker and sometimes metallic in appearance. Only a few forms were produced, mainly cups and dishes, some of which are very large. The decoration is characterized by rouletting, but rims are often grooved and stamps sometimes occur. A short wavy line is found on the rim of some vessels.

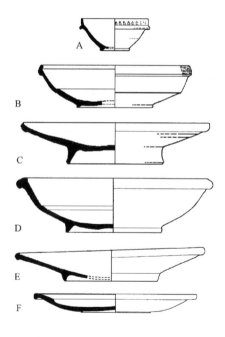

Forms are well dated and a detailed typological sequence exists. Stamped decoration includes floral, religious and geometric designs.

Date: V-VII (or, possibly, VIII)★
Source: Cyprus
Distribution: Throughout the Early
               Byzantine Empire

Egyptian Red Slip Ware (=ERSW)

Three variants of Egyptian Red Slip Ware are found (A, B and C). All can be closely dated and detailed typological sequences have been published.

ERSW A is an imitation of ARSW in a pink or orange-red micaceous fabric with black quartz and larger red inclusions and a matt slip slightly darker than the body. The rims are often discoloured purplish or creamy-white. The lack of

52 Examples of forms of Egyptian and Sagalassos Red Slip Wares. All ERSW except F which is SRSW. After Hayes and Poblome

limestone among the inclusions and darker slip immediately differentiate it from ARSW.

A wide range of forms was produced in ERSW A. Stamped decoration included religious and geometric motifs and the ware is also sometimes rouletted, unlike ARSW.

ERSW B has a coarse red micaceous fabric with a thick, burnished, red slip. In broken surfaces a characteristic reduced purplish core and orange red surfaces are visible, although some pieces can be brownish. Again, a wide range of forms was produced.

ERSW C has a gritty orange or brown fabric, slipped deep red. Limestone, quartz and dark inclusions are visible but little mica. The core is sometimes slightly grey, and the slip slightly micaceous and duller on the interior. The main forms are dishes and bowls. Decoration was usually achieved by grooving, but stamped floral motifs also occur.

Date: A and B V-VII★; C VII+ ★
Source: A — Nile Valley; B — Lower Egypt; C — Egypt
Distribution: A — Egypt, North Africa, Aegean, Anatolia, Palestine; B — Egypt, North Africa; C — Egypt, North Africa, Anatolia, Palestine

Sagalassos Red-Slip ware (=SRSW)

A hard, reddish yellow fabric with small voids. There are no inclusions in most vessels, although in larger vessels a few limestone inclusions can be seen. The darker slip varies in colour but is always smooth. Stamped and rouletted decoration includes geometric and religious designs. A well-dated typological sequence has been established at Sagalassos itself.

Date: <V-VII★
Source: Sagalassos in southern Anatolia
Distribution: Anatolia, Greece, Palestine

Monastic Ware

A gritty buff-red, orange-red or light brown micaceous fabric with limestone inclusions and small dark grits. Unslipped, it is painted with red-brown to brown pigment, sometimes almost purple or black in colour. Closed forms are common but a wide range of forms is known. Geometric, animal, and especially religious, designs occur. This is not an especially well-dated class, with a limited distribution.

Date: V–VI+
Source: Southern Anatolia
Distribution: Anatolia

Egyptian Painted Wares (= Coptic Painted Wares)

A series of painted wares was produced in Egypt in coarse, sometimes gritty, orange or pink, red or red-brown micaceous fabrics with limestone inclusions and voids left from organic (straw?) tempering. The surfaces are covered by pale, often yellow-cream or orange, slip and highly decorated with (usually purple-black or orange-red) painted designs. The designs include human and animal figures, fish and geometric shapes. Often the art of the painted decoration is naturalistic in character, but it may be more abstract. Products included plates, bowls, jars and two-handled flagons.

Red-brown and black painted cream or buff wares found at Carthage, and more widely in at Early Byzantine-period sites (especially towns, as at Thuburbo Maius and Conimbriga) in Tunisia and Spain, may be related to this class, although this was not recognized in their publication. Alternatively, the tradition of manufacturing such painted wares may have been more widespread in North Africa than 'Egyptian' implies.

Date: <V–VII or VIII
Source: Egypt (Abu Mina, Fayoum, Aswan, and probably widely in the Nile Delta). Possibly produced in North Africa outside Egypt?
Distribution: Egypt, possibly North Africa, Palestine and Spain?

Constantinopolitan Whitewares

The earliest variant (CWW1) has a pale brown-orange fabric, occasionally reddish or even grey, with a thin brownish slip. The glaze is olive green or yellow, sometimes brown over interior and lip. There is external glaze only on a minority of later pieces but spots of glaze may be found on the exterior of earlier examples. Scratched decoration includes geometric designs, fish, crosses and (probably religious) inscriptions in Greek letters. The fish designs might also be taken as having a religious meaning, as the fish is a Christian symbol.

CWW2 has an unslipped pure white fabric with a yellowish or greenish glaze. This was extremely common in Constantinople. Ninety per cent of the ninth-century ceramics at the Great Palace excavation (almost entirely unstamped CWW2 and Impressed Ware) were green or yellow glazed. Shapes include dishes and, more commonly, bowls and cups. A characteristic shape was the 'fruit-stand' (pedestal-based shallow bowl). Chafing-dishes, and lids for these and for other shapes, were also made. Hand-formed relief decoration occurs on some lids and chafing-dishes.

53 Examples of forms of Constantinopolitan White Ware from Istanbul. After Hayes and Peschlow et al.

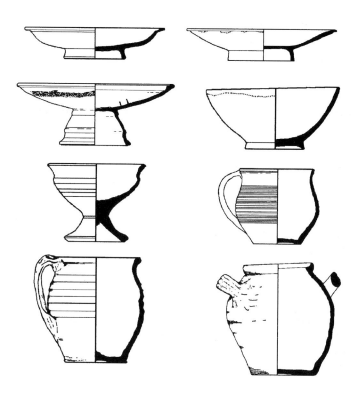

CWW3 has a sandy white hard-fired body with red and grey inclusions reminiscent of Polychrome Ware. A greenish or brownish glaze is used and this can be very thick and glossy.

CWW 4 has a micaceous and gritty sandy white-yellowish or pink fabric, thinly glazed in contrast to CWW 3. The pale greenish-yellowish glaze frequently flakes away, and is normally found on the interior alone. CWW4 can be speckled or painted in green or black (a few — perhaps late — pieces in blue) although the paint is frequently blurred by running.

CWW5 has a gritty micaceous sandy white to yellowish or pink fabric. This has a thin yellowish external glaze, often exhibiting flaking.

Note: I have replaced John Hayes' GWW with CWW while retaining his numerical classification.

Date:	VII-XIII
	CWW1 VII-IX
	CWW2 IX-XII
	CWW3 XI-XII
	CWW4 XII-XIII
	CWW5 XI?-XII
Source:	Constantinople region
Distribution:	Constantinople region, Aegean, Anatolia, Balkans, Crimea, Cyprus, Greece

54 Middle Byzantine Impressed Ware sherd with cross-stamp in the Victoria and Albert Museum

Impressed Ware

At least some Impressed Ware is, as John Hayes has noted, CWW2 decorated with stamped motifs. Nonetheless, it is unclear whether all Impressed Ware was either Constantinopolitan or identical to CWW2, hence the separate entry here. Its fabric is either identical, or very similar, to CWW2. It has a thin red slip, or wash, sometimes used in broad stripes or curvilinear patterns so as to appear in relief, perhaps a characteristic reminiscent of Early Byzantine painted pottery. The key distinguishing feature is the use of stamped designs.

The motifs represented by stamps are not always discernible, but when clear include human and geometric designs, crosses, animals, 'Classical' figures and depictions of saints. One sherd bears what appears to be a representation of a domed church.

Date: IX-XII
Source: Constantinople region, and elsewhere?
Distribution: Constantinople region, Anatolia, Greece

Petal Ware

This is a very characteristic product easily identifiable from body sherds. It is distinguished by the application of 'petals' (oval pellets of clay) as a decorative device to the exterior of the vessel. The fabric and glaze of the body, but not always of the petals (which may be in a red fabric), is identical to that of CWW2, but the use of a red fabric for decoration separates the two. The commonest form is a globular mug with a single handle but closed forms are known. Some examples have alternating glaze colours used for the 'petals' or 'petals' glazed a contrasting colour to the rest of the exterior.

Date: IX-XII
Source: Constantinople region? (manufactured in a CWW2 fabric and common in Istanbul)
Distribution: Constantinople region, Crimea, Greece, Aegean, Anatolia, Balkans

Polychrome Ware

Arguably the finest Middle Byzantine ware, it has a distinctive unslipped sandy grey-white fabric with brown and black particles, hard fired and often discoloured partly or wholly pink. The fabric itself tends to vitrify, making it hard to detect the absence of glaze on its surface. Some vessels have a thin transparent colourless glaze, others an exterior yellow or green glaze. The most distinctive features of Polychrome Ware are the polychrome painted decoration and the use of gold or silver as leaf, or in powder form, in the decoration of some vessels.

Designs include geometric, floral, religious, human, animal and bird motifs, sometimes in a very naturalistic style. Islamic motifs also occur, especially pseudo-Kufic patterns, but this is certainly a Byzantine product. A few pieces have painted Greek inscriptions. Shapes include plates, bowls, one- and two-handled cups, and goblets.

On the basis of coin-dated deposits four groups can be recognized, each with distinct attributes enabling easy identification. Group 1 is distinguished by outlining of designs in black, combined with use of a wide range of colours on a plain white surface. This plain surface is often decorated with red dots. The colours are thinly applied. Forms include very broad rimmed plates and one- or two-handled cups, all with high ring bases. Only Group 1 was produced before *c.*1000, and occurs from the ninth century onward at Istanbul.

Group 2 never has exterior glaze and the background is filled with blocks of thickly applied colour, not red dots. Blue, green and yellow are the most commonly found colours and all tend to be matt. The infilling and lack of dots make it easy to differentiate between groups 1 and 2.

Group 3 has a very restricted range of colours: black, white, yellow, brown and blue. These are thickly applied, and the black and white are glossier than in Groups 1 and 2. The fabric is sometimes sandier and buffer and glaze is again found on the exterior of some vessels.

Group 4 resembles Group 1 but can be easily differentiated from it as it lacks the distinctive outlining of designs found in that Group. Designs are confined to stripes and dots. A distinctive cross motif has dots in each corner. Red is not used and thin brown, blue or green paint is employed. The fabric is finer and harder, but less purely white, than the other groups. Analysis by N.F. Ashbury (for David Talbot Rice) suggested that this fabric contained mica, unlike other Polychrome Ware fabrics, and this may suggest different clay — perhaps from Anatolia — was used.

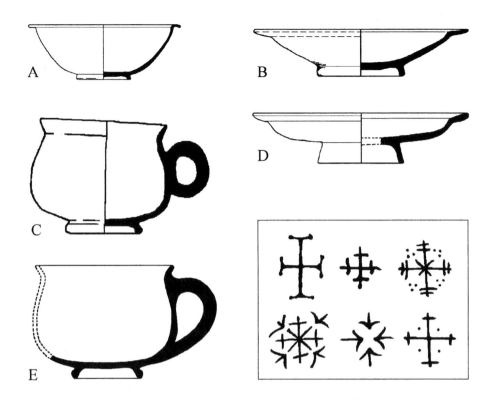

55 *Examples of forms of Polychrome Ware vessels from Corinth and Istanbul. Corinth*
except for B and D from Istanbul. The inset shows examples of cross symbols found on
Polychrome Ware vessels. After Hayes and Peschlow et al.

Polychrome Ware was manufactured in Constantinople during IX-XI as demonstrated by wasters from the monastery of the Great Palace and the churches of
Constantine Lips, the Myrelaion and Kalenderhane. Production also took place at
several centres outside the Byzantine capital after XI, as at Sparta and Corinth, and
in Bulgaria. Polychrome Ware continued in production into at least the early XIII.

Date: IX-XIII
               Group 1 IX-XI
               Group 2 XI+
               Group 3 XII-XIII
               Group 4 XI+
Source: Constantinople region, Corinth, Sparta and elsewhere (in
               Anatolia)?
Distribution: Constantinople region, Aegean, Anatolia, Balkans, Crimea,
               Greece, Palestine (in Crusader contexts)

Polychrome Ware tiles

These are architectural ceramics in the same tradition of painted polychrome glazed pottery and fabrics as Polychrome Ware, and included here for this reason. The tiles are of kaolin- and lead-rich clays containing quartz, iron oxides and other minor components, with clear thin lead glazes. Three main forms exist: a hand-formed flat square tile (sometimes with well-drawn religious designs, often pictures of saints), a semi-tubular curved tile (also hand-formed) and a, perhaps moulded, small half-tubular column with an integral capital.

The decoration is frequently very elaborate and designs include crosses, rosettes, peacocks, saints and probably a (lost) picture of Christ mentioned in a description of the Great Palace. Greek letters are found on the back of some pieces, probably indicating their positions in the buildings they decorated. Although the decoration is sophisticated, the tiles have a restricted palette of red, blue, black and green. One example from Constantinople is known in a red fabric, perhaps a very late imitation.

Imitations of Polychrome Ware tiles (and ceramic icons comprised of these) were also manufactured in courtly contexts in Bulgaria. The imitations are very similar to Byzantine tiles, although distinctive local characteristics can be discerned and some Bulgarian schemes for these tiles may be more elaborate than their Byzantine counterparts — there are even examples from Preslav with lines of continuous text painted onto them before glazing.

Date: IX-XI (+?). Used in Bulgaria (at the Round Church of Preslav) before 907 and incorporated in Cordoba's great mosque in 965
Source: Constantinople (Great Palace?)
Distribution: Constantinople region, Anatolia, Bulgaria, Spain (diplomatic gift)

Imitations of Constantinopolitan Whitewares

Constantinople and other centres produced glazed imitations of the characteristic products of the capital. Imitation CWW2 was manufactured in a red fabric, which was white slipped to copy the white surface of CWW. This is commonly glazed yellow, appearing as brown over the unslipped fabric, and several examples have green and brown painting.

Copies of Impressed Ware were also manufactured in the same fabric as Imitation CWW2. The stamped decoration of the red fabric wares seems more carelessly executed than CWW2 and is usually geometric.

Many glazed whiteware vessels were manufactured outside the capital (for example, they are common at Corinth). These included Imitation Petal Ware bowls, cups and jugs with the 'petals' copied by 'painting in' the shape of each petal in red slip on the white surface of the fabric. This was a minor aspect of painted whiteware production, but interesting in so far as it shows that what is to us the most distinctive feature of Petal Ware was thought worth imitating.

Confusion between Constantinopolitan whitewares and these non-Constantinopolitan products has caused problems in the reporting of Byzantine pottery in the past. The source of all whitewares has usually been assumed to be the capital, but this assumption should be avoided.

Date: XI-XII?
Source: Constantinople region, southern Greece, and perhaps Anatolia
Distribution: Constantinople region, Anatolia, Greece

Measles Ware

A fine red-buff fabric with white inclusions, slipped slightly greenish- or pinkish-white on the interior and on the rims. Only on the cups are all surfaces slipped. A lead glaze was thickly applied to the interior and often to the exterior also, and varies from colourless through yellow to dark-green or brown. This glaze is sometimes identical to that of contemporary Corinthian Fine Sgraffito Ware and the clay is identifiably Peloponnesian, so that although Measles Ware is often claimed to be an Italian import, this is unlikely. Rather, the pieces found in northern Italy might be viewed as Byzantine imports there, as at Venice and Padua, or the class may have been produced both in Greece and Italy.

Shapes are mostly dishes or bowls with fewer cups. The bowls have vertical sides and slightly everted or plain rims, with high ring bases.

The characteristic 'measles' decoration is comprised of red slip-painted dots outlined in sgraffito. Geometric, floral, animal and human designs also occur in sgraffito decoration on these vessels. Suspension marks may indicate that Measles Ware could be displayed by being hung on walls.

Date: XI?-XII
Sources: Southern Greece, possibly Corinth. Italy?
Distribution: Constantinople region, Greece, Italy

56 Examples of forms of Measles Ware from Corinth. After Morgan

Spatter Painted Ware

So-called because it appears to have had red, purple or green paint flicked at it with a brush. The hard fabric is similar to that of Green and Brown Painted Ware. The white slip is covered with a creamy yellow or greenish glaze. There is a wide range of forms for a somewhat rare class, but cups are the most common form and there are fewer dishes and bowls. Chafing-dishes were also produced. The bowls include vertical-rimmed forms with pronounced bases and the cups include ring-handled examples.

Date: XII
Source: Unknown, possibly Corinth
Distribution: Anatolia, Balkans, Greece, Italy, Palestine (Crusader sites)

Fingerprinted Ware

A fine red fabric covered with a yellow, green or brown glaze. It has the distinctive feature that the surface has been decorated by wiping off areas of the glaze with a finger or thumb, leaving a fingerprint. This method was also used to form rows of spots. Forms include plates and bowls. A rare but distinctive class.

Date: XII?
Source: Unknown, possibly Corinth on distribution alone
Distribution: Southern Greece

Imitation Lustre Ware

Imitation Lustre Ware has a pinkish or reddish buff fabric, with a white slip on the interior of plates or bowls and overall on cups. The glaze is glossy and colourless, green or yellow. It usually covers the whole of the vessel. Plates, bowls, cups, jugs and lids were produced. The plates and bowls often have vertical sides and ring bases, and usually plain or slightly flattened rims. Decoration in red slip includes geometric and dotted designs, as well as animal motifs. Some pieces have holes bored through their bases either for suspension or attachment to structural elements as display plates.

Date: XII
Source: Southern Greece, including Corinth
Distribution: Southern Greece

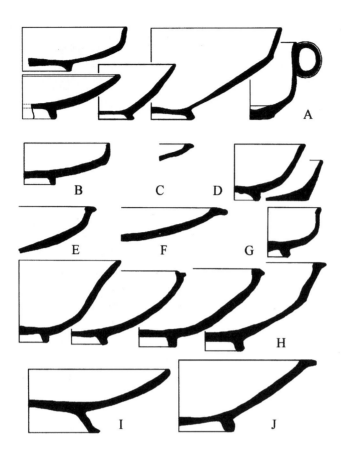

57 Examples of forms of red-painted twelfth-century 'experimental' wares from Corinth. A Spatter Painted Ware; B-H Imitation Lustre Ware; I and J Fingerprinted Ware. After Morgan

Plain Glazed Redwares

Unpainted 'red' fabric pottery with glaze of a single colour and no sgraffito or internal incised decoration. This includes pots in gritty red, brown or grey fabrics, unslipped, and covered with a thick slightly yellowish or colourless lead glaze, consequently appearing mid- or dark-brown and so giving the misnomer 'Brown Glazed Ware'.

By far the most widespread glazed pottery before XII in most of the Byzantine Empire, a variety of shapes was produced. This included cups and lids, although closed forms (especially jugs) are common. Decoration on a minority of pieces includes simple geometric stamps on the exterior and relief modeling, but is usually absent. The jugs include small vessels with a wide range of forms, usually including a globular body and splayed mouth. These seem to have been perfume jugs and have been found with their lead plugs still set (in resin) in place.

Chafing-dishes are common and show a distinct sequence of development. The earliest (Phase A), perhaps belonging to IX, are distinguished by a bowl-shaped body, glazed only on the interior, which joins the base at the bottom of the bowl. There are few perforations in the connecting cylinder or base. A second phase (Phase B) is characterised by dishes with bases joining the bowl at its rim and having a conical boss in

58 Plain Glazed Redware vessel with relief and stamped decoration, probably of Late Byzantine date, in the Victoria and Albert Museum

the centre of the interior of the bowl. These have many perforations in their bowls and applied 'plastic' decoration in the form of human, animal, and mythological figures, is found. Sometimes this seems intended to have a comical effect. In the third phase (Phase C) the body is more rounded and the stand conical. It now joins the body below the rim rather than at it. The tendency for relief decoration is still found, although used more sparingly, and the glaze is still applied to the exterior — this forms an easy way of distinguishing phases A and C.

Date: IX-XII
Source: Southern Greece, Constantinople region and elsewhere?
Distribution: Constantinople region, Greece, Aegean, Anatolia

Green and Brown Painted Ware

'Red' fabric glazed vessels with green and brown painted decoration, sometimes called 'Green and Black Painted Ware' because the brown can be very dark. Shapes include plates, bowls, cups, jugs and chafing-dishes.

In XI and XII, green and brown pigments were applied to a white slip and then covered with an extremely thin clear glaze. This gives a matt 'green and brown' effect and the glaze is only just visible. Later in XII, the pigments were mixed with the glaze prior to application and the colours glossy. The coloured glaze gives a 'swirling' effect of mixed brown and green colours.

In XI decoration usually consisted of stripes, although dotted and geometric designs also occur, and the green and brown paint tends to be equally distributed. A sherd with painted decoration of stripes beneath the glaze is, therefore, likely to be XI.

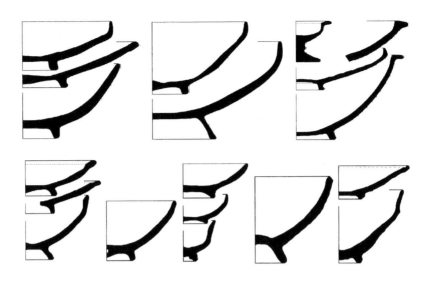

59 Examples of forms of Green and Brown Painted Ware from Corinth. After Morgan

In XII spiral designs appear and designs are often outlined in brown, with green infilling. At this period concentric and medallion designs are first employed, while in XIII green or brown is used monochromatically and dotted designs become common. In the Late Byzantine and Post-Byzantine periods green and brown paint appears randomly applied.

Date: XI-XV+
Source: Greece, and probably elsewhere
Distribution: Constantinople region, Aegean, Anatolia, Balkans, Cyprus, Greece

Fine Sgraffito Ware

Fine red-brown fabrics, usually unslipped and unglazed on the exterior, with scratched decoration cut into the body through a white or pale pink slip. Considerable variation exists in the fabrics used for this class. For example, spectrographic studies of the clay used for Fine Sgraffito Ware from Istanbul, Thessaloniki and Athens suggested that this (and the material from the Pelagonnesos/Alonnesos shipwreck) is distinct from that used for Corinthian Fine Sgraffito Ware products.

Eleventh-century examples (often called 'Duochrome Sgraffito Ware') have light- to mid-yellow, green or brown glazes. These always have a different colour glaze on the interior to exterior. From the twelfth century, the pale yellow or green or deep mid-green glaze is always monochrome. The glazes are always without additional colouring and no pigments were applied to the slip.

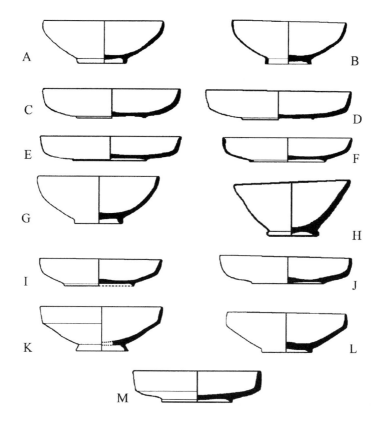

60 Examples of forms of Fine Sgraffito Ware. A, B-F and I Pelagonnesos-Alonessos shipwreck; G Sparta; H and M Argos; J Athens; K Corinth; L Euboea. After Papanikola-Bakirtzi

The sgraffito decoration is characterized by very thin and delicate incision, especially of geometric designs including scrolls. Usually used for shallow plates, other shapes, including closed forms with external sgraffito decoration, are known but rare. One atypical shape is a figure-of-eight-shaped incense burner. Motifs include geometric, mythological, floral and human designs, and pseudo-Kufic decoration is especially common. Rivet holes indicate that some vessels were repaired, probably because they were highly valued.

Date: XII-XIII
Source: Greece including Corinth and Sparta, Constantinople region and elsewhere?
Distribution: Constantinople region, Aegean, Anatolia, Balkans (possibly only Black Sea coast), Crimea, Cyprus, Greece, Italy, Palestine (Crusader sites)

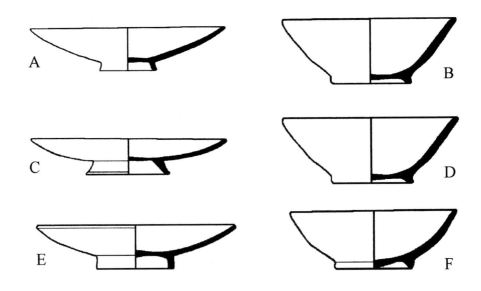

61 Examples of forms of Incised Sgraffito Ware. A Thebes; B Pelagonnesos shipwreck; C and D Thessaloniki; E Chalkidiki; F Argos. After Papanikola-Bakirtzi

Incised Sgraffito Ware

A sgraffito-decorated product with broad-line incisions produced with a gouge rather than delicate stylus. A variety of red, pink or (frequently) brown fabrics were used for the class, often hard and usually with few or no inclusions. The fabric is covered by a white slip and light- to mid-yellow, or light- to mid-green, glaze. This is sometimes very pale, often a whitish yellow. The glaze was applied internally or over the whole vessel.

Decoration in earlier examples focuses on a 'medallion' in the centre of the interior and is mostly geometric, with animals also depicted. On later pieces decoration is unrestrained across the whole of the interior and frequently involves human or animal forms, often employing tendril-like wavy lines radiating toward the rim around a central motif. A typical XII decoration is to add Champleve discs to the second ring of decoration in the interior. Another widespread group, decorated by four large circles with central dots dominating the interior, seems to be XIII, or at earliest late XII.

Date: XII-XIII
Source: Greece including Sparta, Thessaloniki and Corinth, Constantinople region, Cyprus, Balkans and elsewhere?
Distribution: Constantinople region, Anatolia, Aegean, Balkans (especially Bulgaria), Crimea, Cyprus, Greece

62 Examples of forms and decoration of Aegean Ware from Skopelos. After Armstrong/Catling

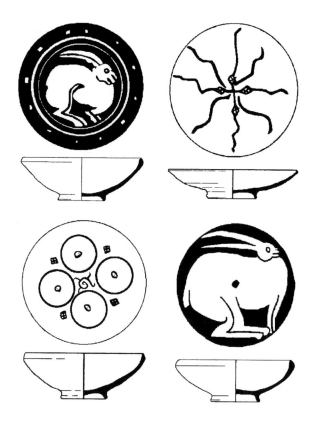

Aegean Ware

A gritty light red-brown/purple-red fabric, covered internally by a white slip and usually with a pale yellow (although sometimes green) glaze, also only on the interior. No other colours of glaze are known, but there is sometimes green glaze splashed on the rim of yellow-glazed examples and in (often symmetrical) dabs elsewhere on the vessel.

Bowls are the only shape and these may have vertical or everted rims. They have a roughly potted ring-base. The vertical rim-form may be earlier, perhaps XII, with everted rims in the XIII, although this is not certain and bevelled rims appear to be present throughout XII-XIII. Aegean Ware is essentially a variant of Incised Sgraffito Ware, in which decoration comprises either a central roundel with animals (often a hare) in relief, within a broad gouged border, or a freer 'sprawling' style of gouged decoration covering the whole interior. Geometric designs, especially compass-drawn circles, are also found.

Date: XII-XIII
Source: Cyprus and Athens region of Greece?
Distribution: Constantinople region, Anatolia, Aegean, Crimea, Cyprus, Greece, Italy, Palestine (Crusader sites)

133

Elaborate Incised Ware

A hard grey-buff or red fabric, with white slip applied overall. Decoration was incised into the body through the slip and the whole vessel covered in green or yellow glaze. When this dried, the incisions were painted with (usually dark brown) glaze before firing. Some vessels seem to have been glazed again and re-fired. Whole areas of slip may be cut away in a way reminiscent of Champleve Ware and infilled in this manner. Elaborate Incised Ware was mostly used for hemispherical bowls, but other shapes were produced.

Decoration includes geometric, animal and human designs. Religious subjects and very elaborate scenes are known. A distinctive 'checkerboard' design of squares in alternating colours, dark and light, is often found, either on the interior base roundel or on the exterior. An 'interlace star' design is extremely common on this class also and the quality of its execution perhaps decreases on later pieces.

Some enigmatic Middle Byzantine and Late Byzantine products may belong to this class, possibly suggesting that its manufacturers were prepared to produce pieces to commission. The class is closely related to the much more common Incised Sgraffito Ware, with which it shares decorative schemes such as the 'checkerboard' and 'interlace star'. Elaborate Incised Ware might well represent a specifically Constantinopolitan 'luxury version' of Incised Sgraffito Ware.

Date: XII-XIII
Source: Constantinople?
Distribution: Constantinople region, northern Greece

Champleve Ware

A hard gritty, light red-brown to light purplish-red fabric, with a white slip. The glaze is light yellow or green, often pale, but sometimes mottled. Shapes include dishes and bowls. The decoration is not scratched into the body, but areas of slip are removed to expose the darker body across broad surfaces prior to glazing. Supplementary decoration was achieved by applying splashes of green glaze.

Decoration includes geometric and animal designs and literary and mytho-logical scenes. Designs either cover the whole interior or form a central motif with a concentric border. Production before *c.*1200 is evidenced at Paphos on Cyprus, although most examples are probably XIII. This class was probably manufactured alongside Fine Sgraffito Ware, as spectrographic analysis has shown they share the same fabrics. Champleve Ware occurs with XIV coins at Kaliakra in Bulgaria, suggesting production beyond Byzantine borders after *c.*1300, but there is no reason to extend the chronology of Byzantine examples beyond this date.

Date: XII-XIII?
Source: Corinth and elsewhere?
Distribution: Constantinople region, Aegean, Anatolia, Balkans, Crimea,
               Cyprus, Greece, Palestine (Crusader sites)

Green and Brown Painted Sgraffito Ware

A soft red-brown fine fabric, slipped in pinkish-buff or cream with transparent-pale cream glaze. The painted decoration is in green and brown on the interior. Shapes are mostly plates and cups.

Sgraffito designs, including geometric, floral and animal motifs, are restricted to a central basal medallion with concentric bands of internal and rim decoration. In XIII streaks and linear designs were added — with brown being more generally used than green — and the fabric has more inclusions, often including sand. A variant with stamped decoration is probably XII.

Date: XII-XIII
Source: Greece, including Pydna
Distribution: Aegean, Balkans, Cyprus, Greece, Italy

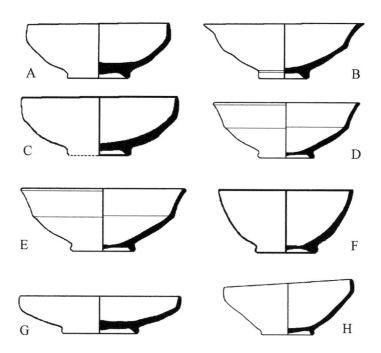

63 Examples of forms of Painted Sgraffito Ware. A Thebes; B Argos; C Thebes; D-E Thessaloniki; F Pydna (Greece); G Euboea; H Greece. After Papanikola-Bakirtzi

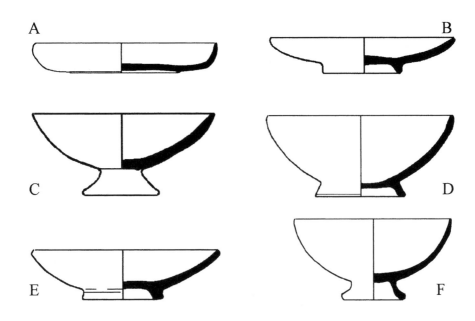

64 Examples of forms of Champleve Ware. A, B and C Thebes; D Sparta; E Near Akraiphnio (Greece); F Greece. After Bakirtzis and Papanikola-Bakirtzi

Coloured Sgraffito Ware (=Late Sgraffito Ware)

Coloured Sgraffito Ware is distinguished by its striking mixture of coloured glazes, with several pigments (usually giving brown and green colours) actually in the glaze itself rather than painted onto the surface prior to glazing. It is characterized by usually thinly potted vessels in a variety of buff, brown to orange-red and red fabrics.

These often have linear decoration cut through white slip into the fabric prior to glazing. Mixing the glazes allows colour from the glaze to more easily enter the incisions than previously. This gives them a darker, often light- to mid-brown, colour, a feature that should not be confused with the deliberately infilled incisions of Elaborate Incised Ware.

Regional variants of Coloured Sgraffito Ware were produced, such as that manufactured in Boetia, with a thick glassy olive-green/yellowish-brown glaze. One especially distinctive, and well-studied, regional group is termed 'Serres Ware', as it was manufactured at Serres in northern Greece during XIII-XIV. This is Coloured Sgraffito Ware with a coarse micaceous red fabric sometimes over-fired grey, white-slipped and brightly yellow- or amber -brown or green glazed to give it very distinctive colouring. The characteristic 'Serres Ware' products were bowls and plates, and few jugs and other closed forms were manufactured.

Date: XII-XV+
Source: Constantinople region, Greece, and elsewhere?

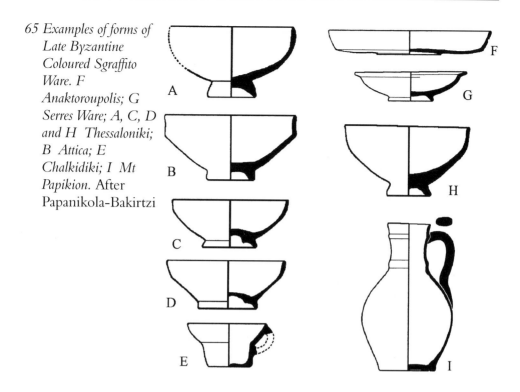

65 Examples of forms of Late Byzantine Coloured Sgraffito Ware. F Anaktoroupolis; G Serres Ware; A, C, D and H Thessaloniki; B Attica; E Chalkidiki; I Mt Papikion. After Papanikola-Bakirtzi

Distribution: Constantinople region, Aegean, Anatolia, Balkans, Crimea, Cyprus, Greece, Italy (one Serres Ware vessel was found in the lagoon at Venice), Palestine (Crusader sites)

Cypriot Sgraffito Ware

A coloured sgraffito variant produced, and mostly used, in Cyprus from at least the early thirteenth century onward. It has a distinctive thick glossy yellow or brown glaze over a pink or white slip, giving a cream or white colour. Characteristic forms include high-sided bowls and cups with tall hollow stems above circular bases. Red or buff fabrics were used and sgraffito decoration is usually contained within a central medallion in the interior base roundel. Earlier examples may be strictly geometrical, but decoration later included figural depictions, notably marriage scenes and female figures. One vessel bears a religious inscription perhaps related to the frequent depiction of these vessels in burials.

Although it is unclear whether any Cypriot Sgraffito Ware was manufactured while the island was under Byzantine rule, the class is usually discussed in relation to Byzantine pottery. It is included here because it continued a Byzantine-period ceramic tradition in relation to current Byzantine fashions in pottery manufacture. The earliest examples may yet prove to date from before Byzantine rule in Cyprus ceased.

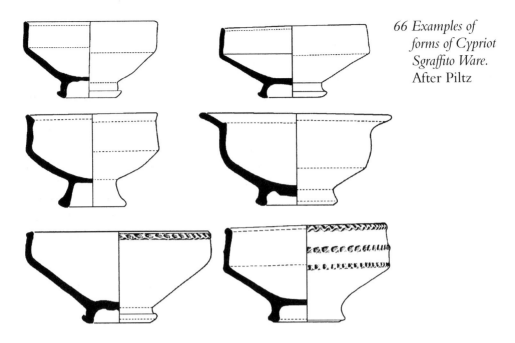

66 Examples of forms of Cypriot Sgraffito Ware. After Piltz

Date: XIII-XV+
Source: Cyprus
Distribution: Cyprus, Greece, Palestine (Crusader sites)

Zeuxippus Ware

When the class was initially identified it seemed to represent a single product with subdivisions. This led to the definition of two 'classes' — Classes I and II — but subsequent work demonstrated that only Class II represents a single product. Class I comprises a range of related pottery, sharing some of the same technical characteristics.

Zeuxippus Ware 'class II' — what might be thought of as 'true Zeuxippus Ware' — has a buff/orange-brown, or even brick red, usually fine hard fabric containing small voids, lime and dark grits. This is white- or cream-slipped (sometimes thickly) on the interior and upper exterior. A distinctive shiny thick glaze covers the slip with a shiny yellow or olive green glaze over the unslipped fabric. The decoration is cut into the slip, not into the body as in other sgraffito wares. A micaceous fabric used for some Zeuxippus-ware derived products may imply an Anatolian source for these.

Designs are in a central basal medallion containing finely cut circles or ovals or a spiral. S-shaped motifs on the centre or side and ovals or triangles on the rim, and club-shaped designs and lines, also occur. Motifs include geometric, human and floral decoration and some extremely elaborate scenes are depicted on Zeuxippus Ware pots from the Crimea, for example a dragon-slaying scene. The presence of rivet holes in some sherds indicates that some pieces were sufficiently well regarded to merit repair.

This ware is the most thinly potted and hardest fired Late Byzantine glazed ware. Both a gouge and stylus were used in its decoration but tripod-stilts were not certainly employed in the manufacture of all Zeuxippus Ware, unlike most Late Byzantine pottery.

'Zeuxippus Ware Class I' in the original classification describes a groups of related but disparate products. 'Class I' was divided into three subdivisions and these give an impression of variation within what can be seen as a broad group of imitations. Class IA was defined as slipped and with colourless glaze, IB having slightly yellow-brown glaze or (often dark) green tinted glaze and IC decorated with circles and spirals in the base of the interior. These all have fine thin red fabrics, with shiny glazes. Many related products seem to have been manufactured.

Date: XIII-XIV
Source: Aegean?, Anatolia?, Italy?, Elsewhere? Not Constantinople on geological grounds
Distribution: Constantinople region, Anatolia, Crimea, Greece, North Africa, and especially northern Italy

Turquoise Glazed Ware

Bowls, plates and jars covered in overall blue-green or greenish blue-grey, 'turquoise', glaze above a pale pink, sometimes gritty fabric. Handled cups, bowls, plates and jugs were manufactured, all of which have exteriors occasionally decorated with purple or brown dots and streaks. Some vessels have 'pie-crust' rims.

Date: XII-XIII?
Source: Sardis area, and elsewhere?
Distribution: Constantinople region, Anatolia

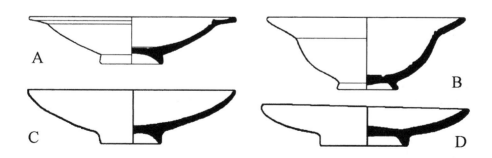

67 Examples of forms of Zeuxippus Ware. A and B bacini Pisa, Italy; C and D Thebes.
Megaw and Papanikola-Bakirtzi

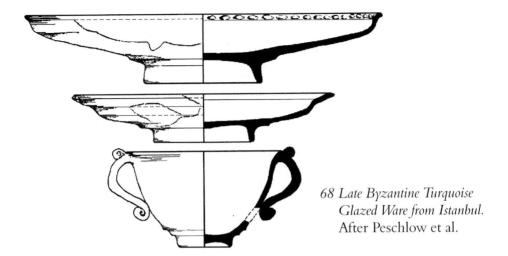

68 Late Byzantine Turquoise Glazed Ware from Istanbul. After Peschlow et al.

Impressed Red Ware

This comprises bowls and plates in a coarse red-grey fabric with dark grits and an overall yellow or green glaze over a white slip. The yellow glaze appears mid-brown above the reddish fabric. Occasionally a cream glaze was used over green and brown paint on this class.

Stamped animal ornament is sometimes found in the centre of the interior (sometimes surrounded by concentric circles of stamped decoration), with a hare design particularly favoured, as on Fine Sgraffito Ware. Other pieces have only geometric designs, extremely similar to those found on CWW2. This may reinforce the likelihood of Byzantine production and offer a hint that the ware begins before XIII. The stamped decoration is limited to a central internal basal medallion. The ware is potentially a crucial link between Middle and Late Byzantine pottery, but few examples come from well-dated contexts.

Date: XII?-XV+?
Source: Unknown, although the Post-Byzantine kilns at Didymoteichon
              produced a version
Distribution: Constantinople region, Greece

Slip-Painted Ware

Easily recognized, even in sherd form, this is a pinkish-buff fabric sometimes reduced to red and with much variation. It is unslipped and usually glazed yellow (often appearing brown over the surface) or green. Shapes include plates, bowls, cups and jugs.

What makes it so distinctive is the use of white slip beneath the glaze in lines, dots, spirals or circles to form the decoration. In XI the glaze was applied exter-

69 Impressed Red Ware in the Victoria and Albert Museum

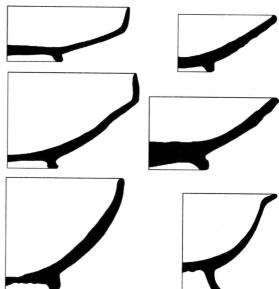

70 Examples of forms of Slip Painted Ware from Corinth. After Morgan

nally and internally, but by XII only on the interior. The slipped decoration also underwent typological changes over time.

Dotted designs are earlier, probably XI. Stripes begin to appear in XII, as does all-over decoration, usually in concentric bands or cross-shape patterns. Motifs are usually geometric but floral and animal designs occur. In XII spiral, pseudo-Kufic motifs and animals are found. A XII variant has the addition of both green and brown glaze to a curvilinear design. On Late Byzantine pieces only geometric designs are found.

On a minority of vessels, relief-decoration, such as segmented U-shaped bands (skeuomorphs of rope handles?) and linear segmented strips, can be found on the exterior. These seem to belong to the phase of linear slip-painted decoration.

Date: Dotted designs XI?, linear designs XII-XV+
Source   Cyprus, Corinth and elsewhere?
Distribution: Constantinople region, Aegean, Anatolia, Balkans, Crimea, Cyprus, Greece, Palestine (on Crusader sites)

Glossary

Some well-known 'everyday' terms are defined here to avoid confusion in their use when applied to specific vessels, in addition to more technical terms. In the text lower case terminology is used for techniques (such as 'sgraffito decoration') when upper case indicates a specific class employing, or named after, this technique (such as 'Fine Sgraffito Ware').

Jar	closed vessel with a depth more than twice its rim diameter, with or without a handle or handles
Bowl	open vessel with a deep body, usually with the body approximately hemispherical or an inverted and truncated cone
Cup	open vessel, usually with one or more handles or a stem supporting a bowl, suitable for use as a drinking vessel
Plate	open vessel with a diameter more than twice its depth
Rouletted	decorated with a wheel-like tool to give a continuous pattern impressed into the surface
Rilled	decorated with continuous, close-set, horizontal grooves
Amphora	vessel with an approximately globular or tubular body, one or more handles attached to the body and a pointed or rounded bottom
Istanbul	large modern city at the junction of Europe and Asia on the Bosphorus
Constantinople	the Byzantine capital city on the same site as the 'old city' of modern Istanbul
Pithos	large vessel with a rounded bottom, usually set into the floor of structure for storage etc.
Jug	vessel with a spout, a flat base and one or more handles
Tile	flat, usually rectangular, semi-tubular or square, ceramic plaque incapable of holding liquid. Usually intended for architectural purposes
Closed Vessel	pot (such as a bottle or amphora) where the upper part is not wholly open (as is a bowl or plate)
Glaze	vitreous material applied to vessel or tile prior to firing in a kiln, in order to give a glassy surface after firing
Slip	thin wash of liquid clay applied to vessel or tile prior to firing in a kiln, in order to give a smooth surface after firing
Fabric	the clay of a vessel or tile, as seen in cross-section if the vessel or tile is broken

Body	synonymous with fabric
Tradition	a manner of action repeated over time, such as a way of making pottery in a particular locality
Class	a group of ceramics sharing sufficient similarities (including at least one unique defining charcteristic separating them from all others) that they may considered together as a single product
Shape	a general category of vessel, such as 'plate', 'jar' or 'bowl'
Type	a subdivision of a class, usually on the basis of variation in form or fabric between it and other members of that class
Form	profile of a vessel or tile, as if seen in cross-section
Typology	the study of the development of form, type or class over time, usually as a means of classification or dating
Skeuomorph	decoration produced by depicting a functional feature in any context where it is rendered devoid of its function, such as the use of clay to depict a rope handle on the exterior of a pot
Sgraffito	decoration using thin lines scratched into the surface
Incised	decoration using broad lines cut into the surface with gouge rather than a thinner lines scratched with a stylus
Ware	a category of pottery
Waster	faulty product discarded in pottery manufacture
Mortarium	grinding bowl or 'mortar' used for preparing food
Tegulation	a tile-like decorative effect of slightly overlapping horizontal ridges
Lustre ware	a technique of producing tin-glazed ceramics
Unguentaria	flasks for holding oil

Note: 'Constantinople' is used in this book to refer to the Byzantine capital, and 'Istanbul' to refer to the modern city on the same site. In the catalogue, 'Constantinople' is used to describe the distribution of pottery to help in relating this pottery to the political geography of the Byzantine Empire.

Notes

Abbreviations

The key works abbreviated here can also be used as an introductory reading list for those wishing to pursue the study of Byzantine pottery further

ARE D.P.S. Peacock and D.F.Williams 1986 *Amphorae and the Roman Economy: an introductory guide* London

BGP D. Talbot Rice 1930 *Byzantine Glazed Pottery* Oxford

BGC D. Papanikola-Bakirtzi (ed.) 1999 *Byzantine Glazed Ceramics. The Art of Sgraffito* Athens

CBP C.H. Morgan 1942 *Corinth XI: The Byzantine Pottery* Cambridge Mass.

BA   V. François 1997 *Bibliographie Analytique Sur La Céramique Byzantine A Glaçure* (= *Varia Anatolica* IX)

LRP J.W. Hayes 1972 *Late Roman Pottery* London; J.W. Hayes 1980 *Supplement to Late Roman Pottery* London (always cited together in this work)

RCB V. Déroche and J.-M.Spieser (eds) 1989 *Recherches Sur la Céramique Byzantine* (= *Bulletin de correspondence hellénique* supplement 18) Athens

SARA J.W. Hayes 1992 *Excavations at Saraçhane in Istanbul Volume 2 The Pottery* Princeton and Washington DC

BT   C. Bakirtzis 1989 *Byzantina Tsoukalolagyna* Athens

Preface

1. Useful general histories of Byzantium are provided by: R. Browning 1992 *The Byzantine Empire* London (2nd ed.); J.Haldon 2000 *Byzantium* Stroud; J.Herrin 1987 *The Formation of Christendom* Oxford; W. Treadgold 1997 *A History of the Byzantine State and Society* Stanford, Calif.
2. For example, it might be used in a similar way to D.P.S. Peacock and D.F. Williams 1986 *Amphorae and the Roman Economy: An introductory guide* London.

1 An introduction to Byzantine pottery

1. A. Cameron 1993 *The Mediterranean World in Late Antiquity AD 395-600* London.
2. C. Mango 1975 *Byzantine Literature as a Distorting Mirror* (Inaugural Lecture) Oxford.
3. For example note the lack of material from low-status secular contexts discussed by: L. Rodley 1994 *Byzantine Art and Architecture: An Introduction* Cambridge.
4. C. Mango 1986 *Byzantine Architecture* London.
5. For the use of ceramics in architecture: K. Tsouris 1988 *The Ceramics and Ornamentation of the Late Byzantine Monuments of North-Western Greece* Kavala; R. Ousterhout 1999 *Master Builders of Byzantium* Princeton.
6. For Byzantine brick building in general: C. Mango 1986 *Byzantine Architecture* London; L. Rodley 1994 *Byzantine Art and Architecture: An Introduction* Cambridge; R. Ousterhout 1999 *Master Builders of Byzantium* Princeton.
7. For examples see: C. Metzger 1981 *Les ampoules à eulogie du Musée du Louvre* Paris; C.J.S. Entwistle 1994 numbers 123-7 in *Byzantium* D. Buckton (ed.), London, 110-13; A. St Clair 1986 numbers 145-52 *Byzantium at Princeton* S. Curcic and A. St Clair 1986 (eds), Princeton, 118-22.
8. SARA, 8-9, 11.

9. The situation is further complicated by the movement of the Roman imperial capital before the foundation of Constantinople, so that the 'Roman Empire' had not been ruled from Rome for substantial periods prior to this. Likewise, Ravenna and Milan served as Western Roman capitals after the foundation of Constantinople.

10. D. Nicol 1993 *The Last Centuries of Byzantium, 1261-1453* (2nd ed.) Cambridge.

11. D. Jacoby (ed.) 1989 *Latins and Greeks in the eastern Mediterranean after 1204* London; P. Lock 1995 *The Franks in the Aegean 1204-1500* London and New York.

12. H. Wallis 1907 *Byzantine Ceramic Art* London; J. Ebersolt 1910 *Catalogue des potéries Byzantines et Anatoliennes du Musée de Constantinople* Istanbul; R.M. Dawkins and J.P. Droop 1910-11 'Byzantine Pottery at Sparta' *Annual of the British School at Athens* 17, 23-8; R. Demangel and E. Mamboury 1939 *Le Quartier des Manganes et la première region de Constantinople* Paris.

13. S. Casson *et al.* 1928 *First Report on the Excavations carried out in and near the Hippodrome of Constantinople in 1927 on behalf of the British Academy* London; D. Talbot Rice 1929 'The Byzantine Pottery' 29-42 in S. Casson *et al. Second Report on the Excavations carried out in and near the Hippodrome of Constantinople in 1928 1927 on behalf of the British Academy* London, 22-35; BGP: D. Talbot Rice 1932 'Byzantine Polychrome Pottery' *Burlington Magazine* 61.357, 281-7. For an application of these advances outside Istanbul: A. Xyngopolous 1933 'Byzantine pottery from Olynthus' in *Olynthus* 5 D.M. Robinson (ed.), Baltimore, 285-92.

14. R.B.K. Stevenson 1947 'The Pottery 1936-7' in *The Great Palace of the Byzantine Emperors, First Report 1935-1938* R.B.K. Stevenson (ed.), Oxford, 31-63; D. Talbot Rice 1958 'The Byzantine Pottery' in *The Great Palace of the Byzantine Emperors, Second Report 1935-1938* D. Talbot Rice (ed.), Edinburgh, 110-20; CBP; A. Frantz 1938 'Middle Byzantine Pottery in Athens' *Hesperia* 7, 429-67. See also: F.O. Waagé 1948 *Antioch-on-the-Orontes* Princeton.

15. CBP

16. For mid- to late twentieth-century work: BA. See also: J. Herrin 1982 'La Céramique' in *Splendeur de Byzance*; J. Lafontaine-Dosogne (ed.), Brussels, 225-39; J. Hayes 1997 'Ceramics of the Byzantine Period'in *The Oxford Encyclopedia of Archaeology in the Near East* E.M. Meyers (ed.), Oxford and New York 417-75.

17. J.W. Hayes 1972 *Late Roman Pottery* London and J.W. Hayes 1980 *Supplement to Late Roman Pottery* London; J.W. Hayes 1992 *Excavations at Saraçhane in Istanbul Volume 2 The Pottery* Princeton and Washington DC.

18. For example: ARE; SARA. See also: S.J. Keay 1984 *Late Roman Amphorae in the Western Mediterranean* Oxford; P. Reynolds 1995 *Trade in the Western Mediterranean AD 400-700: the ceramic evidence* Oxford; E. Campbell 1996 The archaeological evidence for external contacts: imports, trade and economy in Celtic Britain AD 400-800' in *External Contacts and the Economy of Late Roman and Post-Roman Britain* K.R. Dark (ed.), Woodbridge, 83-96.

19. J. Magness 1993 *Jerusalem Ceramic Chronology circa 200-800 CE* Sheffield; C. Williams 1989 *Anemurium: the Roman and Early Byzantine Pottery* (= *Subsidia Mediaevalia* 16).

20. For examples: L. Paroli (ed.) 1992 *La ceramica invertriata tardoantica e altomedievale in Italia* Florence; S. Gelichi (ed.) 1993 *La Ceramica Nel Mondo Bizantino Tra XI E XV Secolo E I Suoi Rapporti Con L'Italia* Florence; G.R. Sanders 1987 'An Assemblage of Frankish Pottery from Corinth' *Hesperia* 56, 159-95; T. Wilson 1987 *Ceramic Art of the Italian Renaissance* London; S. Gelichi 1984 'Roulette Ware' *Medieval Ceramics* 8, 47-58.

21. G. Nikolapoloulos 1981 'Céramiques encastées d'anciennes églises de Grèce' *Faenza* 67, 166-7; A.H.S. Megaw 1964 'Glazed bowls in Byzantine Churches' *Deltion Tes Christiantikes Achaiologikes Hetaireias* 4, 145-62; D. Pringle 1986 'Pottery as Evidence of Trade in the Crusader States' in *I Communi Italiani Nel Regno Crociato Di Gerusalemme* G. Airaldi and B.Z. Kedar (eds), Genoa, 449-75; A.J. Boas 1994 'The Import of Western Ceramics to the Latin Kingdom of Jersualem' *Israel Exploration Journal* XLIV, 102-22; E. Stern 1995 'Exports to the Latin East of Cypriot Manufactured Glazed Pottery in the 12th-13th Century' in *Cyprus and The Crusades* N. Coureas and J. Riley-Smith (eds), Nicosia, 325-36; D. Papanikola-Bakirtzi 1986 *Medieval Cypriot Pottery in the Pierides Foundation Museum* Larnaca; E. Piltz 1996 *The Von Post Collection of Cypriot Late Byzantine Glazed Pottery* (= *Studies in Mediterrnean Archaeology* CXIX).
22. For example: H. Maguire (ed.) 1997 *Materials Analysis of Byzantine Pottery* Washington DC; A.H.S. Megaw and R.E. Jones 1983 'Byzantine and Allied Pottery: a contribution by chemical analysis to problems of origin and distribution' *Annual of the British School at Athens* 78, 235-263.

2 Byzantine coarse-wares: 1000 years of continuity in pottery production?

1. BT.
2. For this and the next paragraph: BT; S. Tsuji (ed.) 1995 *The Survey of Early Byzantine Sites in Oludeniz Area (Lycia, Turkey). The First Preliminary Report* Osaka; S. Crawford 1990 *The Byzantine Shops at Sardis* Cambridge Mass.; J. Hayes 1997 'Ceramics of the Byzantine Period' in *The Oxford Encyclopedia of Archaeology in the Near East* E.M. Meyers (ed.), Oxford and New York 417-75.
3. SARA; C. Williams 1989 *Anemurium: the Roman and Early Byzantine Pottery* (= *Subsidia Mediaevalia* 16).
4. R. Degeest 2000 *The Common Wares of Sagalassos* Turnhout.
5. C. Williams 1989 *Anemurium: the Roman and Early Byzantine Pottery* (= *Subsidia Mediaevalia* 16); H.W. Catling 1972 'An Early Byzantine Pottery Factory at Dhiorios in Cyprus' *Levant* 4 1-82; J. Boardman 1989 'The Pottery' in *Byzantine Emporio* M. Balance, J. Boardman, S. Corbett and S. Hood (eds), London, 88-121.
6. S.C. Williams 1989 *Anemurium: the Roman and Early Byzantine Pottery* (= *Subsidia Mediaevalia* 16). For examples of imports of Byzantine coarse-ware to the West: L. Vallauri 1994 'Les céramiques communes importées' in *L'Oppidum de Saint-Blaise du Ve au VIIe s.* G. Démains D'Archimbaud (ed.) Paris 116-17, K.R. Dark 2000 *Britain and the End of the Roman Empire* Stroud, esp. ch. 3.
7. J. Magness 1993 *Jerusalem Ceramic Chronology circa 200-800 CE* Sheffield.
8. For the fourth century, and earlier Roman, background: J. Hayes 1997 'Ceramics of the Hellenistic and Roman Periods' in *The Oxford Encyclopedia of Archaeology in the Near East* E.M. Meyers (ed.), Oxford and New York 469-71; J.W. Hayes 1997 *Handbook of Mediterranean Roman Pottery* London.
9. C. Williams 1989 *Anemurium: the Roman and Early Byzantine Pottery* (= *Subsidia Mediaevalia* 16). J.W. Hayes 1967 'North Syrian Mortaria' *Hesperia* 36, 337-47. Stratigraphical evidence available only since Hayes' 1967 paper supports their continued use into the fifth and sixth centuries.
10. In addition to ARE and SARA see: J.A. Riley 1979 'The Coarse Pottery from Berenice' in *Excavations at Sidi Khrebish, Benghazi (Berenice)* (= *Libya Antiqua*, Supplement 5) J.A. Lloyd (ed.), volume 2, 91-467; J.A. Riley 1981 'The pottery from the cisterns 1977.1, 1977.2 and 1977.3' in *Excavations at Carthage 1977, Conducted by the University of Michigan* VI ed. J. Humphrey, 85-124; P. Arthur

1986 'Amphorae and the Byzantine World' in *Recherches sur les Amphores Grecques* (= *Bulletin de Correspondence Hellénique* supplement 13) J.-Y. Empereur and Y.Garlan (eds), Athens, 655-60; J.-Y. Empereur and M.Picon 1989 'Les Régions de Productions d'Amphores Impériales en Méditeranée Orientale' in *Amphores Romaines et Histoire Économique: Dix Ans de Recerche*, Rome, 223-48; M. Sciallano and P. Sibella 1994 *Amphores. Comment les identifier?* Édisud 2nd edition; S. Kingsley 1994-5 'Bag-Shaped Amphorae and Byzantine Trade: Expanding Horizons' *Bulletin of the Anglo-Israel Society* 14, 39-56; J. Freed 1995 'The late series of Tunisian cylindrical amphoras at Carthage' *Journal of Roman Archaeology* 8, 155-91; G. Majcherek 1995 'Gazan Amphorae: Typology Reconsidered' in *Hellenistic and Roman Pottery in the Eastern Mediterranean — Advances in Scientific Studies* H. Meyza and J. Mlynarczyk (eds), Warsaw, 163-78; P.G. Van Alfen 1996 'New Light on the 7th-c. Yassı Ada Shipwreck: Capacities and Standard Sizes of LR1 Amphoras' *Journal of Roman Archaeology* 9, 189-213.

11. For example, D.M. Bailey 1988 *A Catalogue of the Lamps in the British Museum. III Roman Provincial Lamps* London. See also: A. Karivieri 1996 *The Athenian Lamp Industry in Late Antiquity* Helsiniki; C. Trost and M.-C. Hellmann 1996 *Lampes Antiques du département des Monnaies, Médailles et Antiques III, Fonds Générales lampes Chrétiennes* Paris; M. Barbera and R. Petriaggi 1993 *La Lucerne Tardo-Antiche Di Produzione Africana* Rome; S. Luffreda 1989 *Lucerne bizantine in Terra santa con inscrizione in Greco* Jerusalem; S. Loffreda 1995 *Lucerne Cristiane Della Terra Santa* Jerusalem; A. Ennabli 1976 *Lampes Chrétiennes de Tunisie (Musées de Bardo et de Carthages)* Paris.

12. BT. For Middle Byzantine coarse-wares from western Anatolia: J.-M. Spieser 1996 *Die Byzantinische Aus der Stadtgrabung Von Pergamenische* Berlin; J.-M. Spieser 1985 'La céramique: nouvelle approche' in *Le Grand Atlas de l'Archaéologie* Paris, 144-5.

13. For the Byzantine ceramics of Thasos: C. Abadie-Reynal and J.-P. Sodini 1992 *La Céramique Paléochrétienne De Thasos (Aliki, Delkos, Fouilles Anciennes)* Athens and Paris; V. François 1995 *La céramique Byzantine à Thasos* (= *Études Thasiennes* XVI).

14. P. Armstrong 1996 'The Byzantine and Ottoman Pottery' in *Continuity and Change in a Greek Rural Landscape: The Laconia Survey, II* W.G. Cavanagh, J. Crouwel, R.W.V. Catling and G. Shipley (eds), London, 125-40; T. Stillwell-Mackay 1967 'More Byzantine and Frankish Pottery from Corinth' *Hesperia* 36, 249-320; G.R. Sanders 1993 'Excavations at Sparta: The Roman Stoa, Preliminary Report, part 1 (1988-91)' *Annual of the British School at Athens* 88, 251-86.

15. 'Slavic' pottery is discussed in: G.R. Sanders 1993 'Excavations at Sparta: The Roman Stoa, Preliminary Report, part 1 (1988-91)' *Annual of the British School at Athens* 88, 251-86. For comparable material from the north Balkans: R.K. Falkner 1999 'The Pottery' in A.G. Poulter 1999 *Nicopolis ad Istrum. A Roman to Early Byzantine City. The Pottery and Glass* London, 55-296, esp. 91, 107, 112, plates VII and VIII and 260-3; T.S. Ivancan 2001 *Early Medieval Pottery in Northern Croatia* Oxford. For the problem of correlating ethnic identity and pottery groups in Byzantine-period Greece: J. Vroom 2000 'Piecing together the Past: Survey Pottery and Deserted Settlements in Medieval Boeotia (Greece)' in *Byzanz als Raum: zu Methoden und Inhalten der historischen Geographie des östlichen Mittelmeeraumes* K. Belke (ed.), Vienna, 245-60.

16. N. Günsenin 1989 'Recherches sur les amphores byzantines dans les musées turcs' in RCB, 267-76. See also: C. Bakirtzis 1989 'Byzantine Amphorae' in RCB, 73-7.

17. BT; CBP; T. Stillwell-Mackay 1967 'More Byzantine and Frankish Pottery from Corinth' *Hesperia* 36, 249-320; G.R. Sanders 1987 'An Assemblage of

Frankish Pottery from Corinth' *Hesperia* 56, 159-95; G.R. Sanders 2000 'New Relative and Absolute Chronologies for 9th to 13th Century Glazed Wares at Corinth: Methodology and Social Conclusions' in *Byzanz als Raum: zu Methoden und Inhalten der historischen Geographie des östlichen Mittelmeeraumes* K. Belke (ed.), Vienna, 153-74.

18. G.R. Sanders 1987 'An Assemblage of Frankish Pottery from Corinth' *Hesperia* 56, 159-95; G.R. Sanders 2000 'New Relative and Absolute Chronologies for 9th to 13th Century Glazed Wares at Corinth: Methodology and Social Conclusions' in *Byzanz als Raum: zu Methoden und Inhalten der historischen Geographie des östlichen Mittelmeeraumes* ed. K. Belke Vienna, 153-74; P. Armstrong 1989 'Lakonian Amphorae' in RCB, 185-8.

19. N. Günsenin 1989 'Recherches sur les amphores byzantines dans les musées turcs' in RCB, 267-76; G.R. Sanders 1987 'An Assemblage of Frankish Pottery from Corinth' *Hesperia* 56, 159-95.

3 Byzantine fine-wares: pottery as periodization

1. The standard work is LRP. See also: A. Martin 1998 'La sigillata focese (Phocaean Red Slip/Late Roman C Ware) in *Ceramica in Italia: VI-VII Secolo* L. Sagui (ed.) Florence, 109-22; J. Poblome 1999 *Sagalassos Red Slip ware Typology and Chronology* Turnhout. The ongoing series of excavation reports for Carthage offer detailed chronological revisions to Hayes' dating.

2. P.M. Watson 1989 'Jerash Bowls: Study of a Provincial Group of Byzantine Fine Ware' in *Jerash Archaeological Project* vol. 2 *Fouilles de Jérash, 1984-88* F. Zayadine (ed.), Paris 223-61. On Egyptian pottery of the fifth to seventh centuries: W. Godlewski (ed.) 1990 *Coptic and Nubian Pottery* Warsaw; M. Egloff 1977 *Kellia: La Poterie Copte* Geneva (3 vols.); B. Johnson 1981 *Pottery from Karanis* Ann Arbor.

3. C. Williams 1989 *Anemurium: the Roman and Early Byzantine Pottery* (= *Subsidia Mediaevalia* 16). On copying in general: J.-P. Sodini 2000 'Productions et échanges dans le monde protobyzantin (IVe-VIIe s.): Le cas de la céramique' in *Byzanz als Raum: zu Methoden und Inhalten der historischen Geographie des östlichen Mittelmeeraumes* K. Belke (ed.), Vienna, 181-208.

4. SARA; J.W. Hayes 1997 'Réflexions sur les céramiques paléochrétiennes d'Orient et leurs liens avec l'Occident' in *La Cérmamique Médiévale en Méditerranée* (ed.) G.D. d'Archimbaud Aix-en-Provence, 49-52; G.F. Bass 1982 'The Pottery' in *Yassı Ada II, A Seventh Century Byzantine Shipwreck* G.F. Bass and F.H. Van Doorninck (eds), College Station, 155-88.

5. I am grateful to The British Museum for the opportunity to inspect the Deir 'Ain Abata sherds before publication. C. Williams 1989 *Anemurium: the Roman and Early Byzantine Pottery* (= *Subsidia Mediaevalia* 16).

6. On pottery in Early Byzantine Syria: F.O. Waagé 1948 *Antioch-on-the-Orontes* Princeton; D. Orssaud 1980 'La céramique' in 'Déhès (Syrie du Nord) Campagnes I-III (1976-1978): recherches sur l'habitat rural' *Syrie* LVII, 234-66.

7. S. Crawford 1990 *The Byzantine Shops at Sardis* Cambridge Mass. esp. 96-7; C. Williams 1989 *Anemurium: the Roman and Early Byzantine Pottery* (= *Subsidia Mediaevalia* 16).

8. G. Kuzmanov 1998 'Spätantike Glasierte Keramik Aus Bulgarien' *Archaeologia Bulgarica* II.1, 81-95.

9. For this and the next paragraph: SARA.

10. For Forum Ware: D.B. Whitehouse 1965 'Forum Ware: A Distinctive Type of Early Medieval Glazed Pottery in the Roman Campagna' *Medieval Archaeology*, 55-63; D.B. Whitehouse 1967 'The Medieval Glazed Pottery of Lazio'

Proceedings of the British School at Rome 35, 40-86; R. Hodges and H. Whitehouse 1986 'San Vincenzo al Volturno and the origins of Medieval Pottery in Italy' *La ceramic medievale nel mediterrano occidente* (no editor cited) Florence, 14-26.

11. C. Williams 1989 *Anemurium: the Roman and Early Byzantine Pottery* (= *Subsidia Mediaevalia* 16).

12. SARA

13. The account of Islamic pottery in this and following paragraphs is based on: J.A. Sauer and J. Magness 1997 'Ceramics of the Islamic Period' in *The Oxford Encyclopedia of Archaeology in the Near East* E.M. Meyers (ed.), Oxford and New York, 475-9; V. Porter 1981 *Medieval Syrian Pottery* Oxford; P. Ballet 1997 'De l'empire romain à la conquête arabe. Les productions céramiques égyptiennes' in *La Céramique Médiévale en Méditerranée* G.D. d'Archimbaud (ed.), Aix-en-Provence, 53-62.

14. O. Watson 1985 *Persian Lustre Ware* London; S.R. Canby 'Islamic Lustreware'in *Pottery in the Making* I. Freestone and D. Gaimster (eds), London, 110-15.

15. J.A. Sauer and J. Magness 1997 'Ceramics of the Islamic Period' in *The Oxford Encyclopedia of Archaeology in the Near East* E.M. Meyers (ed.), Oxford and New York, 475-9; P. Ballet 1997 'De l'empire romain à la conquête arabe. Les productions céramiques égyptiennes' in *La Céramique Médiévale en Méditerranée* G.D. d'Archimbaud (ed.), Aix-en-Provence, 53-62; J.P. Sodini and E. Villeneuve 1990/1993 'Le passage de la céramique Byzantine à la céramique omeyyade' in *La Syrie de Byzance à l'Islam VIIe-VIIIe siècles* P. Canivet and J.P. Rey-Coquais (eds), Paris (1990) and Damascus (1993), 195-198.

16. D. Talbot Rice 1937 'Persian Elements in the Arts of Neighbouring Countries' *Journal of the Royal Central Asian Society* XXIV, 385-96; D. Talbot Rice 'The Pottery of Byzantium and the Islamic world' in *Studies in Islamic Art and Architecture in honour of K.A.C. Cresswell* C. Geddes (ed.), Cairo, 194-236.

17. SARA.

18. The whiteware copies were first noticed by Talbot Rice (in BGP) and Morgan (in CBP), but others from Sparta exist in the Victoria and Albert Museum, identified by the author and from Iznik, recognised by Veronique François. For her important work on Iznik see: V. François 1996 'Céramiques ottomane de tradition byzantine d'Iznik' *Anatolia Antiqua* 4, 231-45; V. François 1997 'Les ateliers de c éramique byzantine de Nicée/Iznik et leur production, Xe-début Xie siècle' *Bulletin de Correspondence Hellénique* 121/I, 423-58. On redware copies see: G.R. Sanders 2000 'New Relative and Absolute Chronologies for 9th to 13th Century Glazed Wares at Corinth: Methodology and Social Conclusions' in *Byzanz als Raum: zu Methoden und Inhalten der historischen Geographie des östlichen Mittelmeeraumes* K. Belke (ed.), Vienna, 153-74.

19. The following description and discussion of Polychrome Ware is based on: BGP; CBP; D. Talbot Rice 1954 'Byzantine Polychrome Pottery. A Survey of Recent Discoveries' *Cahiers Archéologiques* VII, 69-74; P. Verdier 1983 'The Tiles of Nicomedia' in *Okeanos* (= *Harvard Ukrainian Studies* VI), 632-6; R.B. Mason and M. Mango 1995 '"The Glazed Tiles of Nicomedia" in Bithynia, Constantinople and Elsewhere' in *Constantinople and its Hinterland* C. Mango and G. Dagron (eds), Aldershot, 313-31; C. Vogt 1990 *La Céramique Byzantine du Musée du Louvre* Paris.

20. For Theophilus: C.R. Dodwell (ed. and trans.) 1986 *Theophilus Presbyter, The Various Arts* Oxford. See also, M. De Boüard 1974 'Observations on the treatise of Eraclius, *De Colouribus et artibus Romanorum*' in *Medieval Pottery from Excavations* V.I. Evison, H. Hodges and J.G. Hurst (eds.) London, 67-76 (73).

21. The discussion of Proto-Mailoica pottery here is based on: CBP; D. Whitehouse 1980 'Proto-Maiolica' *Faenza* 66, 1.6, 77-87; S.P. Uggeri (ed.) 1997 *La Protomaiolica Bilancio E Aggiornamenti* Florence.

22. This section is based on BGC except where otherwise referenced.

23. A.H.S. Megaw 1975 'An Early Thirteenth-Century Aegean Glazed Ware' in *Studies in Memory of David Talbot Rice* G. Robertson and G. Henderson (eds), Edinburgh, 34-45; P. Armstrong 1991 'A Group of Byzantine Bowls from Skopelos' *Oxford Journal of Archaeology* 10.3, 335-47.

24. This discussion is based on information from: CBP; BGP; R.B.K. Stevenson 1947 'The Pottery 1936-7' in *The Great Palace of the Byzantine Emperors, First Report 1935-1938* R.B.K. Stevenson (ed.), Oxford, 31-63; J.W. Hayes 1981 'The Excavated Pottery from the Bodrum Camii' in C.L. Striker *The Myrelaion (Bodrum Camii) in Istanbul* Princeton, 36-41, 43-4.

25. K.R. Dark 1994 'The Constantine Bowl: A Late Byzantine Diplomatic Gift?' *The Burlington Magazine* CXXXVI 1101, 829-31.

26. This account of tenth- to thirteenth-century Islamic pottery is based on: J. Irwin 1997 *Islamic Art* London; J.W. Allan 1991 *Islamic Ceramics* Oxford; J.W. Allan 1971 *Medieval Middle Eastern Pottery* Oxford; V. Porter 1995 *Islamic Tiles* London.

27. BGC; CBP; SARA and H. Maguire (ed.) 1997 *Materials Analysis of Byzantine Pottery* Washington DC; A.H.S. Megaw and R.E. Jones 1983 'Byzantine and Allied Pottery: a contribution by chemical analysis to problems of origin and distribution' *Annual of the British School at Athens* 78, 235-63.

28. CBP; SARA; R.B.K. Stevenson 1947 'The Pottery 1936-7' in *The Great Palace of the Byzantine Emperors, First Report 1935-1938* R.B.K. Stevenson (ed.), Oxford, 31-6.

29. BGC; D. Papanikola-Bakirtzis 1986 'The Tripod Stilts of Byzantine and Post-Byzantine Pottery' in *Ametos. Volume in Honour of Professor Manolis Andronikos* Thessaloniki, 641-48; D. Papanikola-Bakirtzis, E. Dauterman Maguire and H. Maguire (with contributions by C. Bakirtzis and S. Wisseman) *Ceramic Art from Byzantine Serres* (= *Illinois Byzantine Studies* III) Urbana and Chicago.

30. This and the following paragraph are based on: S. Gelichi (ed.) 1993 *La Ceramica Nel Mondo Bizantino Tra XI E XV Secolo E I Suoi Rapporti Con L'Italia* Florence. For the character of East-West relations in this period see also: A. Laiou 1980-1 'The Byzantine economy in the Mediterranean trade system: thirteenth-fifteenth centuries' *Dumbarton Oaks Papers* 34-5, 177-222; D.M. Nicol 1988 *Byzantium and Venice* Cambridge.

31. BGP; SARA; R.B.K. Stevenson 1947 'The Pottery 1936-7' in *The Great Palace of the Byzantine Emperors, First Report 1935-1938* R.B.K. Stevenson (ed.), Oxford, 31-6; U. Peschlow (with catalogue and illustrations by G. and S. Sişmanoğlu) 1977-8 'Byzantische Keramik aus Istanbul. Ein Fundkomplex bei der Irenkirche' *Istanbuler Mitteilungen*, 27-8, 363-414.

32. J.A. Scott and D.C. Kamilli 1981 'Late Byzantine glazed pottery from Sardis' *Actes due XVè Congrès International d'Études Byzantines* Athens, 679-96. See also: V. François 1998 'Céramiques importées à Byzance: une quasi absence' *Byzantinoslavica* 58 (1998), 387-404; V. François 1998 'L'arrivée de l'Islam en Anatolie, un vecteur de diffusion de la céramique chinoise' *Annales Islamologiques* XXXII, 41-7.

33. BGC; D. Pringle 1986 'Pottery as Evidence of Trade in the Crusader States' in *I Communi Italiani Nel Regno Crociato Di Gerusalemme* G. Airaldi and B.Z. Kedar (eds), Genoa, 449-75; A.J. Boas 1994 'The Import of Western Ceramics to the Latin Kingdom of Jersulaem' *Israel Exploration Journal* XLIV, 102-22; E. Stern 1995 'Exports to the Latin East of Cypriot Manufactured Glazed Pottery in the 12th-13th Century' in *Cyprus and The Crusades* N. Coureas and J. Riley-Smith (eds), Nicosia, 325-36.

34. BGC and BAS; A.H.S. Megaw 1968 'Zeuxippus Ware' *Annual of the British School at Athens* 63, 67-88; A.H.S. Megaw 1989 'Zeuxippus Ware Again' in RCB, 259-66; P. Armstrong 1992 'Zeuxippus derivative bowls from Sparta' in *PHILOLAKON. Lakonian studies in honour of Hector Catling* ed. J.M. Sanders, Athens, 1-9; T. Makarova 1972 *Céramique vernissée de l'ancienne Russie* Moscow; A. Bank 1977 *Byzantine Art in the Collections of the USSR* Leningrad.
35. BGC.

4 The manufacture and marketing of Byzantine pottery

1. D.P.S. Peacock 1982 *Pottery in the Roman world: an ethnoarchaeological approach* Harlow. On the archaeology of fine-ware production centres: M. Mackensen 1998 'Centres of African Red Slip Ware Production in Tunisia from the Late 5th to the 7th Centuries' in *Ceramica in Italia: VI-VII Secolo* L. Sagui (ed.) Florence, 23-39.
2. K.R. Dark 1996 'Proto-industrialization and the end of the Roman economy' in *External Contacts and the Economy of Late Roman and Post-Roman Britain* K.R. Dark (ed.), Woodbridge, 1-21.
3. P. Grossmann 1991 'Abu Mina' in *The Coptic Encyclopedia* I New York, 24-9; S. Hill 2000 'Çiftlik 2000' *Anatolian Archaeology* 6, 3-4.
4. H.W. Catling 1972 'An Early Byzantine Pottery Factory at Dhiorios in Cyprus' *Levant* 4 1-82.
5. J. Herrin 1996 'Ceramics' in *The Dictionary of Art* J. Turner (ed.), London, 631-5.
6. CBP.
7. J. Herrin 1996 'Ceramics' in *The Dictionary of Art* J. Turner (ed.), London, 631-5.
8. *Ibid.*
9. BGC; N. Günsenin 1993 'Ganos. Centre de production d'amphores à l'époque Byzantine' *Anatolia Antiqua* II, 93-201.
10. K.R. Dark forthcoming report on Great Palace pottery.
11. T. Totev 1987 'L'atelier de céramique peinte du monastère royal de Preslav' *Cahiers Archéologiques* 35, 65-80.
12. G.R. Sanders 2000 'New Relative and Absolute Chronologies for 9th to 13th Century Glazed Wares at Corinth: Methodology and Social Conclusions' in *Byzanz als Raum: zu Methoden und Inhalten der historischen Geographie des östlichen Mittelmeeraumes* K. Belke (ed.), Vienna, 153-74.
13. For this and the following two paragraphs: C. Vogt 1993 'Technologie des céramiques Byzantines á glaçure d'époque Comnène. Les décors incisés: les outils et leur traces' *Cahiers Archéologiques* 41, 99-110; P. Armstrong, H. Hatcher and M. Tite 1997 'Changes in Byzantine Glazing Technology From The Ninth To Thirteenth Centuries' in *La Cérmamique Médiévale en Méditerranée* G.D. d'Archimbaud (ed.), Aix-en-Provence, 225-30; G.R. Sanders 2000 'New Relative and Absolute Chronologies for 9th to 13th Century Glazed Wares at Corinth: Methodology and Social Conclusions' in *Byzanz als Raum: zu Methoden und Inhalten der historischen Geographie des östlichen Mittelmeeraumes* K.Belke (ed.), Vienna, 153-74.
14. G.R. Sanders 1993 'Excavations at Sparta: The Roman Stoa, Preliminary Report, part 1 (1988-91)' *Annual of the British School at Athens* 88, 251-86.
15. D. Papanikola-Bakirtzis, E. Dauterman Maguire and H. Maguire (with contributions by C. Bakirtzis and S. Wisseman) *Ceramic Art from Byzantine Serres* (= *Illinois Byzantine Studies* III) Urbana and Chicago. For the 'ethnoarchaeological' approach to pottery making: D.P.S. Peacock 1982 *Pottery in the Roman world: an ethnoarchaeological approach* Harlow. For twentieth-century 'traditional' pottery manufacture in the eastern Mediterranean: R. Hampe and A. Winter 1962 *Bei*

Töpfern und Töpferinnen in Kreta, Mesenien und Zypern Mainz; H. Blitzer 1990 'Koroneika: Storage-jar Production and Trade in the Traditional Aegean' *Hesperia* 59, 675-711.

16.CBP.

17.Important exceptions include: V. François 1997 'Sur La Circulation Des Céramiques Byzantines En Méditerranée Orientale Et Occidentale' in *La Cérmaique Médiévale en Méditerranée* G.D. d'Archimbaud (ed.), Aix-en-Provence, 231-6; J.-M. Spieser 19 'La céramique Byzantine médiévale' in *Hommes et Richesses dans l'empire Byzantin* vol. 2, V. Kravari, J. Lefort and C. Morrisson (eds), Paris, 249-60. For discussions of Early Byzantine trade using pottery as evidence see: C. Abadie-Reynal 1989 'Céramique et commerce dans le bassin Egéen du IVe au VIIe siècle' in *Hommes et Richesses dans l'empire Byzantin* vol. 1, V. Kravari, J. Lefort and C. Morrisson (eds), Paris, 143-162; J.-P.Sodini 2000 'Productions et échanges dans le monde protobyzantin (IVe-VIIe s.): Le cas de la céramique' in *Byzanz als Raum: zu Methoden und Inhalten der historischen Geographie des östlichen Mittelmeeraumes* K. Belke (ed.), Vienna, 181-208; S. Kingsley and M. Decker (eds) 2001 *Economy and Exchange in the East Mediterranean during Late Antiquity* Oxford.

18.S. Kingsley 1994-5 'Bag-Shaped Amphorae and Byzantine Trade: Expanding Horizons' *Bulletin of the Anglo-Israel Society* 14, 39-56.

19.For this and the following three paragraphs: *Ibid.*; P.M. Watson 1995 'Ceramic Evidence for Egyptian links with Northern Jordan in the Sixth-Eighth Centuries AD' in *Trade, Contact and the Movement of Peoples in the Eastern Mediterrranean: Studies in Honour of J. Basil Hennessy* S. Bourke and J.-P. Descoeurdres (eds), Sydney, 303-20.

20.On Mediterranean maritime archaeology: A.J. Parker 1992 *Ancient Shipwrecks of the Mediterranean and the Roman Provinces* Oxford.

21.A. Bowman 1996 'Post-Roman imports in Britain and Ireland: a maritime perspective' in *External Contacts and the Economy of Late Roman and Post-Roman Britain* K.R. Dark (ed.), Woodbridge, 97-108, esp. 104-8.

22.K.R. Dark (ed.) 1996 *External Contacts and the Economy of Late Roman and Post-Roman Britain*, Woodbridge; A. Sazanov 1997 'Les amphores de l'Antiquité tardive et du Moyen Age: continuité ou rupture? Le cas de la Mer Noire' in *La Céramique Médiévale en Méditerranée* G.D. d'Archimbaud (ed.), Aix-en-Provence, 87-102.

23.S. Kingsley 1994-5 'Bag-Shaped Amphorae and Byzantine Trade: Expanding Horizons' *Bulletin of the Anglo-Israel Society* 14, 39-56.

24.This discussion is based on: K.R. Dark 'Early Byzantine Mercantile Communities in the West' in *Through a Glass Brightly. Studies in Honour of David Buckton* C. Entwistle (ed.) (forthcoming); K.R. Dark 1994 *Civitas to Kingdom* London, 211.

25.A. Sazanov 1997 'Les amphores de l'Antiquité tardive et du Moyen Age: continuité ou rupture? Le cas de la Mer Noire' in *La Céramique Médiévale en Méditerranée* (ed.) G.D. d'Archimbaud Aix-en- Provence, 87-102.

26.BGC. On the Byzantine economy in this period: A. Harvey 1989 *Economic Expansion in the Byzantine Empire, 900-1200* Cambridge; M. Angold 1997 *The Byzantine Empire 1025-1204* (2nd ed.) London and New York, chs 5 and 13; J. Haldon 2000 *Byzantium* Stroud chs 3-5.

27.G.R. Sanders 2000 'New Relative and Absolute Chronologies for 9th to 13th Century Glazed Wares at Corinth: Methodology and Social Conclusions' in *Byzanz als Raum: zu Methoden und Inhalten der historischen Geographie des östlichen Mittelmeeraumes* K. Belke (ed.), Vienna, 153-74.

28. BGP; N. Günsenin 2001 'L'Epave De Çamalti Burnu I (Isle de Marmara, Proconnese): Resultats Des Campagnes 1998-2000' *Anatolia Antiqua* IX, 117-33.
29. Discussion of these monograms here is based on: BGP; BA; BGC; R. Demangel and E. Mamboury 1939 *Le Quartier des Manganes et la première region de Constantinople* Paris; C. Bakirtzis 1989 'Byzantine Amphorae' in RCB, 73-7; C. Bakirtzis 1997 'Amphora Stamp' (catalogue number 179) in *The Glory of Byzantium: art and culture of the Middle Byzantine era A.D. 843-1261* H.C. Evans and W.D. Wixom (eds), New York, 180.
30. BGC.

5 Ceramics as a source for reconstructing Byzantine culture

1. For example, at Sardis: S. Crawford 1990 *The Byzantine Shops at Sardis* Cambridge Mass.
2. CBP.
3. CBP; E. Dauterman Maguire 1997 'Ceramic Arts of Everyday Life' in *The Glory of Byzantium: art and culture of the Middle Byzantine era A.D. 843-1261* (eds.) H.C. Evans and W.D. Wixom New York, 254-71; J. Durand *et al.* 1992 *Byzance* Paris, 396-7.
4. M. Frank 1941 'Akritas and the Dragons' *Hesperia* 10, 9-13; J.A. Notopoulos 1964 'Akritan Ikonography on Byzantine Pottery' *Hesperia* XXXIII.2 108-33.
5. CBP.
6. Byzantine burial practices have been the subject of a recent doctoral study by Dr Eric Ivison, but at the time of writing this remains unpublished. In his work, Dr Ivison has independently drawn attention to use of ceramic vessels in burial practice. For the falsity of this misconception in the West: K.R. Dark 2000 *Britain and the End of the Roman Empire* Stroud, 78.
7. A. Vavyopolou-Charitonidou 1989 'Ceramique trouvée en offrande dans des tombes Byzantines tardives de l'Hippodrome de Thessalonique'in RCB 209-26.
8. J. Travlos and A. Frantz 1965 'The Church of St Dionysios the Areopagite and the Palace of the Archbishop of Athens in the 16th Century' *Hesperia* XXXIV.3, 157-202; S.T. Parker 1994 'A Late Roman soldier's grave by the Dead Sea *Annual of the Department of Antiquities of Jordan* 38, 317-24.
9. SARA; E. Parman 1989 'The Pottery from St.John's Basilica at Ephesos' in RCB, 277-89.
10. D. Kurtz and J. Boardman 1971 *Greek Burial Customs* New York.
11. LRP.
12. K. Weitzmann 1976 *The Monastery of St.Catherine at Mount Sinai vol. 1, The Icons: From the Sixth to the Tenth Century* Princeton.
13. On the scarcity of pre-Iconoclast religious art in Constaninople, for example: T.F. Mathews 1998 *The Art of Byzantium* New York, 105.
14. L. Rodley 1985 *Cave Monasteries of Byzantine Cappadocia* Cambridge; A. Wharton Epstein 1986 *Tokali Kilise: Tenth-Century Metropolitan Art in Byzantine Cappadocia* Washington DC.
15. To judge from the Impressed Ware sherds illustrated or described in BGP; CBP; SARA; H. Wallis 1907 *Byzantine Ceramic Art* London; J. Ebersolt 1910 *Catalogue des potéries Byzantines et Anatoliennes du Musée de Constantinople* Istanbul; R. Demangel and E. Mamboury 1939 *Le Quartier des Manganes et la prémière region de Constantinople* Paris; S. Casson *et al.* 1928 *First Report on the Excavations carried out in and near the Hippodrome of Constantinople in 1927 on behalf of the British Academy* London; R.B.K. Stevenson 1947 'The Pottery 1936-7' in *The Great Palace of the Byzantine Emperors, First Report 1935-1938* R.B.K. Stevenson (ed.), Oxford, 31-63 and seen by the author in Istanbul, and at The British Museum and the Victoria and Albert Museum in London.

16. For examples: BGP; CBP; BGC; and 'Ceramics' in *Byzantine and Post-Byzantine Art* M. Archeimastou-Potamianou (ed.), Athens, 228-49.

17. The groups were first proposed by Charles Morgan in CBP. See also: P. Armstrong 1989 'Some Byzantine and later settlements in Eastern Phocis' *Annual of the British School at Athens* 84, 1-42.

18. BGP; BA; C. Bakirtzis and D. Papanikola-Bakirtzi 1981 'De la céramique byzantine en glaçure à Thessalonique' *Byzantino-Bulgarica* 7, 421-36; D. Papanikola-Bakirtzis 1987 'The Palaeologan Glazed Pottery of Thessaloniki' *Recueil des rapports du Ive Colloque serbo-grec sur l'art Thessalonique et les pays balkaniques et courants spirituals au XIVe siècle, 1985* Belgrade, 193-304.

19. In an as yet unpublished lecture at the International Congress of Byzantine Studies held in 2001 at Paris.

20. LRP.

21. C. Mango 1980 *Byzantium* London, especially ch. 1.

22. BGP; SARA; J. Herrin 1996 'Ceramics' in *The Dictionary of Art* J. Turner (ed.), 631-5 London; J.W. Hayes 1997 'Réflexions sur les céramiques paléochrétiennes d'Orient et leurs liens avec l'Occident' in *La Cérmamique Médiévale en Méditerranée* G.D. d'Archimbaud (ed.), Aix-en-Provence, 49-52.

23. Although centaurs and other mythological animals occur in Islamic art of this period, it is unclear whether these were derived from Byzantine prototypes, from the shared Classical artistic heritage of the Byzantine and Islamic worlds, or if they were the models for the use of mythological images on Byzantine pottery.

24. A point illustrated by: M. Sciallano and P. Sibella 1994 *Amphores. Comment les identifier?* Édisud (2nd ed).

25. For example: K. Weitzmann 1981 *The Classical Heritage in Byzantine and Near Eastern Art* London.

26. E. Ettinghausen 1954 'Byzantine Tiles from the Basilika in the Topkapu Sarayi and Saint John of Studios (463 A.D.)' *Cahiers Archaeologique* VII, 79-88; P. Verdier 1983 'The Tiles of Nicomedia' in *Okeanos* (= *Harvard Ukrainian Studies* VI), 632-6; R.B. Mason and M. Mango 1995 '"The Glazed Tiles of Nicomedia" in Bithynia, Constantinople and Elsewhere' in *Constantinople and its Hinterland* C. Mango and G. Dagron (eds), Aldershot, 313-31.

27. The site is not yet fully published, but a brief journalistic account with colour video footage and still photographs of the frescos is on the World Wide Web: http:news.bbc.co.uk/hi/english/world/europe/newsid_151000/151554.stm. The latest report available at the time of writing is: A.Pasinli 1999 'Büyük Saray Bölgesinde Sultanahmet Eski Cezaevi Bahçesindeki 1997-1998 Kazi Çalismalarına ait Rappor' *Kurtama Kazıları Sempozyumu Ankara* s.100 8/9.

28. H. Maguire (ed.) 1997 *Materials Analysis of Byzantine Pottery* Washington DC. A major monograph in preparation on this material was not available at the time of writing: S.E. Gerstel and J.A. Lauffenberger (eds.) 2001 *A Lost Art Rediscovered. The Architectural Ceramics of Byzantium* Baltimore and Philadelphia.

29. For this and the following paragraph: BGP; K. Miiatev 1936 *Preslavskata Keramika/ Die Keramk von Preslav* (= *Monumenta Artis Bulgariae* 4); I. Akrabova-Zhandova 1968 'La Decorazione ceramica nell'architectura bulgara dei secoli IX e X' *Corsi di Cultura sull'Arte Ravennate e Bizantina* 15, 7-19; I. Akrabova-Zhandova 1975 'Preslav Inlaid Ceramics' in *Studies in Memory of David Talbot Rice* G. Robertson and G. Henderson (eds), Edinburgh, 25-33; A. Chilingirov 1979 *Die Kunst de christlichen Mittelalters in Bulgarien* Munich; V.N. Zalesskaya 1984 'Nouvelles découvertes de céramique peinte byzantine du Xe siècle' *Cahiers Archéologiques* 32, 49-62; T. Totev 1987 'L'atelier de céramique peinte du monastère royal de Preslav' *Cahiers Archéologiques* 35, 65-80; J.D. Alchermes

1997 'The Bulgarians' in *The Glory of Byzantium: art and culture of the Middle Byzantine era A.D. 843-1261* H.C. Evans and W.D. Wixom (eds), New York, - 335; E. Schwartz 1982 'Medieval ceramic in Bulgaria' *Byzantinoslavica* 43, 45-50.

30. R.B. Mason and M. Mango 1995 '"The Glazed Tiles of Nicomedia" in Bithynia, Constantinople and Elsewhere' in *Constantinople and its Hinterland* (eds.) C. Mango and G. Dagron Aldershot, 313-31.

31. K.R. Dark 1994 'The Constantine Bowl: A Late Byzantine Diplomatic Gift?' *The Burlington Magazine* CXXXVI 1101, 829-31.

6 Conclusion: the end of the Byzantine period and beyond

1. Armstrong 1989 'Some Byzantine and later settlements in Eastern Phocis' *Annual of the British School at Athens* 84, 1-42. For Cyprus: D. Papanikola-Bakirtzi 1986 *Medieval Cypriot Pottery in the Pierides Foundation Museum* Larnaca; E. Piltz 1996 *The Von Post Collection of Cypriot Late Byzantine Glazed Pottery* (= *Studies in Mediterrnean Archaeology* CXIX) and D. Papanikola-Bakirtzi 1986 *Medieval Cypriot Pottery in the Pierides Foundation Museum* Lanarca. For a recent account of the end of this tradition in Cyprus: I. Ionas 2001 *Traditional Pottery and Potters in Cyprus. The disappearance of an ancient craft industry in the 19th and 20th centuries* (= *University of Birmingham Byzantine and Ottoman Monographs* vol. 6).

2. BGC; BA.

3. M. Whittow 2001. As yet unpublished lecture at 'Archaeology of Late Antiquity Conference', University of Oxford.

4. BGC.

5. This description is based on: C. Bakirtzis 1980 'Didymoteichon: Un centre de céramique post-byzantine' *Balkan Studies* 21.1 147-53. On the local Byzantine background: C. Bakirtzis 1992 'Byzantine glazed pottery from western Thrace' *Eighteenth (1992) Byzantine Studies Conference Abstracts* Urbana-Champaign, USA, 27-8. See also BGC.

6. V. François 1996 'Céramiques ottomane de tradition byzantine d'Iznik' *Anatolia Antiqua* 4, 231-45; V. François 1997 'Les ateliers de c éramique byzantine de Nicée/Iznik et leur production, Xe-début Xie siècle' *Bulletin de Correspondence Hellénique* 121/I, 423-58. See also: O. Aslanapa, S. Yetkin and A. Altun 1989 *The Iznik Tile Kiln Excavations* Istanbul.

Index

Index of pottery classes and related subjects: see also general index
Pages printed **bold** contain illustrations